The Biblical Basis
for Evangelization

Theological Reflections based
on an African Experience

The Biblical Basis for Evangelization

Theological Reflections based on an African Experience

J.N.K. Mugambi

Nairobi
OXFORD UNIVERSITY PRESS
1989

Oxford University Press

OXFORD GLASGOW NEW YORK
TORONTO MELBOURNE AUCKLAND
PETALING JAYA SINGAPORE HONG KONG TOKYO
DELHI BOMBAY CALCUTTA MADRAS KARACHI
NAIROBI DAR ES SALAAM CAPE TOWN

and assocites in
BERLIN IBADAN

ISBN 019 572700 2

OXFORD is a trademark of Oxford University Press

Cover design by Justice Mugaki

Published by Oxford University Press, Eastern Africa, Science House,
Monrovia Street, P.O. Box 72532, Nairobi, Kenya
and printed by General Printers Ltd., P.O. Box 18001,
Homa Bay Road, Nairobi, Kenya.

Contents

Introduction 1

Chapter One:
The Biblical Basis for Evangelization 5

Chapter Two:
Christian Theology as Contextual Response 22

Chapter Three:
Christian Response to Dehumanizing Situations 39

Chapter Four:
Response of the Church to Crises in Africa 52

Chapter Five:
New Orientations in the Ecumenical Sharing of
    Resources 58

Chapter Six:
Some Problems of Christian Theological Education
    in Africa 69

Chapter Seven:
The Social Context of Christianity in Colonial and
    Post-colonial Africa 77

Chapter Eight:
Christian Baptism and the Naming of Persons 92

Chapter Nine:
The Primary Business of the Church 101

Chapter Ten:
Mission as the be-all and end-all of the Church 110

Chapter Eleven:
The Cultural Context of Mission 120

Appendix 1:... 133
Appendix 2:... 134
Appendix 3:... 135
Appendix 4:... 136
Appendix 5:... 137
Appendix 6:... 138
Appendix 7:... 139
Appendix 8:... 140
Appendix 9:... 141
Index*:*... 143

Author's Preface and Acknowledgements

The establishment of Christianity in Africa south of the Sahara is one of the most significant processes of modern history. This process was facilitated by the Modern Christian Missionary enterprise, organized through societies and organizations which, until 1961, operated in Africa in total autonomy and without reference to the churches with which they were associated back home. In that year, the Third Assembly of the World Council of Churches in New Delhi launched a new relationship when the International Missionary Council was incorporated into the WCC as the Division of World Mission and Evangelism.

Despite the centrality of the Bible as the frame of reference for the Christian faith, it appears that much of missionary activity in Africa has been only remotely related to the demands of the Gospel. For this reason, many African Christians felt and still feel obliged to follow the scriptures rather than the missionaries who introduced the Bible in the first place. The crisis of authority in Christian Mission has led to competition and conflict in some situations while in others it has facilitated ecumenical dialogue and co-operation.

This book will, hopefully, stimulate further discussion on the Biblical basis for evangelization, particularly in the African historical context. The book discusses topics which are of specific interest and relevance in contemporary Africa.

Acknowledgement is extended to all those who have directly and indirectly contributed to the development of the ideas contained herein, including those scholars whose works are cited or alluded to. The list would be too long, and perhaps never exhaustive, and so a general appreciation is herewith expressed. Many people have debated the insights presented here, and it is through their encouragement that it is considered worthwhile to share these reflections more widely.

The chapters in this book were first articulated as lectures to a wide variety of audiences, ranging from International Travelling Seminars of American theology students, consultations of ecumenically oriented African Christian students, workshops of lay and ordained participants under the auspices of the All Africa Conference of Churches, consultations on Faith and Order and Ecumenical Sharing Resources convened by the World Council of Churches, staff consultations of the National Council of Churches, and a Conference of Bible College Tutors of the Anglican Church in Kenya. I would like to extend my appreciation to all those international friends and professional colleagues who challenged me to respond to these themes identified as priorities for the attention of the church in the contemporary period. I also thank the hundreds of participants in these consultations, whose critical remarks helped me to recast the original versions into revised publishable form.

In particular, I would like to thank the staff of the National Council Churches of Kenya, especially the General Secretary, the Revd Samuel Kobia and the Deputy General Secretary, Mr Richard Odeng'. Not only did they invite me to share my reflections and research with them in exchange for their searching questions and criticism; they also insisted that arrangements be made to make the material available in print. I am grateful to them for their interest and encouragement.

I also thank the staff of the All Africa Conference of Churches, particularly the Revd José Chipenda, for taking a keen interest in my concern for the need to raise the level of theological awareness in Africa. The title of this book is lifted from the theme of one of the consultations that the AACC convened, which I was invited to address. It is my hope that the book as a whole will be of constructive help to those within and without the ecumenical movement in Africa and abroad.

I must also express my gratitude to the staff of the World Student Christian Federation, particularly Mr Manuel Quintero of the Inter-Regional Office in Geneva and the Rev Steve Muin, Regional Secretary for Africa. With confidence and boldness they invited me to share my research, reflection and experience with a new generation of ecumenically minded students, nearly a decade after I, myself, had left (in 1976) the service of the WSCF as the Theology Secretary for Africa. The WSCF consultation on the theme "Africa: Beyond Crises of Survival" in October 1985 challenged me to reflect critically on the responses of the church to crises in Africa. I hope the

WSCF will find in this book much food for thought.

For twenty years I have been acquainted with various aspects of the World Council of Churches and the exposure to, and interaction with, committed professional friends and colleagues in all continents has been deeply satisfying and theologically enriching. This exposure has enabled me to grow out of my cultural and religious cocoon, to appreciate the universal appeal and relevance of the Gospel and the necessity to interpret and apply the universal demands of the Good News in particular cultural, religious and historical contexts. In particular, I thank Dr Lukas Vischer, former Director of the Faith and Order Commission, and Dr Geiko Muller-Fahrenholz who for a time was Executive Secretary in the Commission. The chapter on baptism was written during preparations for the Lima Conference where the *Baptism Eucharist and Ministry* consensus document was approved in 1982. Although we did not always approach issues from a common perspective, I appreciated their affirmation of the unity of the Christian faith despite the difficulty of articulating that unity. The Office for the Ecumenical Sharing of Resources invited me to contribute some insights on new orientations for sharing, and the chapter on this theme was prepared in that context.

Prof. Robert Evans invited me to address his International Travelling Seminars in Nairobi, first from McCormick Theological Seminary in Chicago, then from Hartford Theological Seminary in Connecticut. The chapter on theology as contextual response was prepared for one of those seminars. I thank him for the invitation and for the challenging questions raised by him and his students.

The chapter on the social context of Christianity was prepared in the context of an invitation to address the International Travelling Seminar from Yale Divinity School. I thank the organizers of the seminar for inviting me, and for responding with searching questions and reflections.

The Provincial Board of Theological Education of the Anglican Church in Kenya invited me to address the Bible College tutors from all dioceses in February 1988, and the chapter on Problems of Theological Education was prepared in that context, although drafts of it had been written earlier. I thank the Revd Graham Kings and the Revd Mark Russsel-Smith for facilitating my participation in that conference. I also thank Dr Gerald Collier who came from Durham, U.K., to serve with me as resource persons for the conference.

The reader is invited to join this international and ecumenical community of enquirers, in the company of which the author has been theologically, philosophically and professionally nourished.

I warmly thank my family for allowing me to sometimes delay their own priorities in order to read, write, beat deadlines and attend the numerous meetings.

Finally I must thank the publishers, especially Mr A.K. Ismaily and Mrs Beatrice Omari, for facilitating speedy processing of this book through the publication process. Mr N.G. Ngulukulu's editorial advice was admirable. What remains now is the reader's part to read, reflect and act accordingly.

Introduction

THE CHALLENGE OF AFRICAN CHURCHES IN THE TWENTY-FIRST CENTURY

Peace, Love and Unity

I would like to introduce this book by referring the reader to four others that have been published about the problems of the Church and of society in Kenya during the last thirty to forty years. Perhaps it is best to begin with the book entitled, *Kenya African Nationalism: Nyayo Philosophy and Principles,* which was recently published. I would urge each one of my readers to make sure that he reads it: not once but several times, because it states the context within which anyone currently working in Kenya has to operate. It is very important that we understand this particular setting in order to view whatever we do within this framework. I think it is an interesting and readable book, well produced and reasonably priced. The credit is to the author, and also to the publisher in making it very readily available at a very affordable price in a paperback edition.[1]

The Centre Cannot Hold

The other reference is a book by the historian Roland Oliver, entitled *The Missionary Factor in East Africa*[2] which was published in the early 1950s. It is a book that has become a classic text book, a very important reference work for anyone who wishes to understand the history of mission in East Africa and the social and political context within which the Church has developed in parts of Africa. I wish to suggest that anyone who wants to take serious account of the mission of the Church in East Africa should read the book.

More specifically I would like to refer to a challenge which Roland Oliver pointed out when he was writing his book. In the preface to the first edition, written around 1951, he made an observation about a vital question of the Churches' leadership, to which no reassuring answer could be given. It concerned the utter failure of the Churches ever since the 1920s to attract into the Christian ministry even a handful of the best educated East Africans. During the first three decades of the colonial period, this had not been so. Of the first literate generation of East Africans, the elites became either chiefs or churchmen. But with the development of secondary education, and with the widening of secular opportunities, the Churches began to be outpaced in the competition for the best educated men. With the beginnings of higher education, the situation grew even more serious.

In the early 50s, Oliver observed, when University College of East Africa began to put forth its first graduates, that there was still not a single Ordained Minister in any of the Churches who had received even the beginnings of a secondary education in any of the lay schools. If the Roman Catholic seminaries provided a partial exception to this rule, it was only by pursuing a policy of isolating possible candidates for the ministry from a very early age. During the 1940s, while hundreds of East Africans were studying in the universities of Europe, Asia and North America, a tiny trickle of Roman Catholics clergy was flowing to the Gregorian University. But other Christian denominations still lacked a single African graduate in the Ordained Ministry. The elite which won political independence and now exercises political control is thus an entirely secular elite with which the clergy can scarcely communicate effectively.

In the second edition published in 1970, Oliver observed that, the Church's work is most evident in the villages but the life in the towns, and especially in the capitals, has passed it by. As he wrote in 1951, the danger is that under the stress of political and social change, *organized Christianity may start to disintegrate at the centre while it is expanding at the circumference.* The challenge that is posed to us now as we prepare to enter the twenty-first century, is this: Twenty years after the 2nd edition and forty years after the book was first published — Is the situation different? Has it improved? Is it worse? What can be done? Whatever conclusion you draw is important.

A Call for Theological Maturity

The 3rd book that I wish to refer to is by the Kenyan scholar, Prof. John Mbiti. When he published his *New Testament Eschatology in an African*

Background,[3] in 1971, he noted in his conclusion that the Church in East Africa and in Africa as a whole, has "come into existence and has grown evangelistically but not *theologically".*[4]

This evangelical growth also concerns numerical strength. The Church has grown very much in terms of numbers of members, sponsored schools, clinics and dispensaries. In terms of the physical out-reach, the Church has grown tremendously. But as far as theological growth is concerned, it appears that the Church has not yet grown significantly. And so the search goes on for an African Christian theology; but whatever the results, they will not descend on a plate from the sky. Most embarrassingly, the very Church which has produced the majority of present African leaders and thinkers, has itself hardly any theologians, whether African or expatriate. The tragedy goes further back in that with only a few exceptions, the missionaries who established Christianity in the past two centuries were not theologians.

In 1968, Mbiti observed, the Churches could not count more than half a dozen African theologians engaged in theological output, teaching, preaching and writing. The question we ought to ask ourselves today, 20 years later, is this — What is the situation now? Is the Church beginning to grow theologically in order to match its numerical out-reach and growth? That is a challenge to which the National Council of Churches need address itself, particularly because those who have had the honour and the privilege to serve within the structures of the ecumenical movement are perhaps best placed to make a contribution in the direction suggested by Roland Oliver and John Mbiti.

The Quest for an African Christian Theology of Mission

The last reference is again from John Mbiti. In one of the chapters of a book published in Nairobi by Oxford University Press, in 1986 — *The Bible and Theology in African Christianity,*[5] he talks about mission out-reach in African theology. He goes on to say: "Our first observation is one of great disappointment. Up to the present, there is virtually nothing published by African theologians on the mission of the Church in Africa. This is shocking, but it is true according to the extensive research which I have undertaken in preparation for this analysis. What there is in plenty, however, is the opinion of Africans about foreign missions on our continent. This means that we have a considerable number of books and articles about the work of foreign missionaries including the evangelism, education, medical and welfare services. But African theology as such is virtually silent on the active participation in mission by and from the Church which is rooted in Africa."[6]

If Prof. Mbiti is right, what are we going to do about it? This is a challenge to all of us. In the course of preparing this publication, I thought that this perhaps would be a forum where we should suggest the direction in which we should be moving in order to address ourselves particularly to this challenge.

NOTES

1. Daniel T. Arap Moi, *Kenya African Nationalism: Nyayo Philosophy and Principles,* London: Macmillan, 1986.

2. Roland Oliver, *The Missionary Factor in East Africa,* London: Longman, 1952, 2nd ed. 1970.

3. J.S. Mbiti, *New Testament Eschatology in an African Background,* London: Oxford University Press, 1971.

4. *Op.Cit.,* p. 188.

5. J.S. Mbiti, *The Bible and Theology in African Christianity,* Nairobi: Oxford University Press, 1986.

6. Op.Cit., p. 177.

Chapter One

THE BIBLICAL BASIS FOR EVANGELIZATION

The Christian Faith as a Scriptural Religion

The Christian faith is a scriptural religion. It shares this characteristic with Judaism (Torah), Islam (the Qu'ran), Hinduism (the Vedas and other scriptures developed therefrom) and Buddhism (the teachings of Gautama Buddha).[1] In Christianity the Bible is the basic source from which essential Christian doctrines are derived. Among Christians, especially in the Protestant tradition, the Bible is the primary authority through which doctrinal and theological questions are resolved. It comprises the Old and the New Testaments, and both these sections are ecumenically agreed to be complementary.[2] Thus without the New Testament, the Old Testament is not fully intelligible.[3]

The Christian faith is founded on Jesus Christ, who commented on the Old Testament as follows: 'Think not that I have come to abolish the law and the prophets, I have come not to abolish them but to fulfil them. For truly, I say to you, till heaven and earth pass away, not an iota, not a dot, will pass from the law until all is accomplished. Whoever then relaxes one of the least of these commandments and teaches men so, shall be called least in the kingdom of heaven, but he who does them and teaches them shall be called great in the kingdom of heaven. For unless your righteousness exceeds that of the scribes and Pharisees, you will never enter the kingdom of heaven.' (Matt, 5:17–20).

The fixing of the Biblical Canon took a long time to settle. Since the Reformation, some of the books which the Roman Catholic Church had included in the Canon were regarded by Protestant Churches to be appocryphal. Today there are versions of the Bible which include the appocryphal books and some which do not. However, all the main branches of the Christian faith — Orthodox, Catholic, Anglican, Protestant and even the African 'Independent Churches — are agreed that the Bible is central to the Christian faith. The question as to which books in it are most important within each Christian denomination is a secondary point with regard to this affirmation of the centrality of the Bible in Christianity.[4]

This fact of the centrality of the Bible in the Christian faith implies that any concerns with which the Church may be involved should be related to the basic teaching of the Bible. Since the time when Martin Luther emphasized the priority of 'Justification by faith' over salvation through good works, the faith-works polarity has been a point of doctrinal contention among Christians. The polarity is as old as the Christian faith, and this can be confirmed by reading the epistles of Paul on the one hand and the epistle of James on the other. It points to the broad variety of Biblical interpretations and emphases which are observable in the many denominations of the Christian faith. At the same time, such differences in emphasis and interpretation are indicative of the profound depth of teaching contained in the Bible: it is much more profound than all the denominational emphases and interpretations put together. A comprehensive combination of all the denominational Biblical scholarship would not exhaust the depth of the teaching of the Bible. If this were not the case, the Bible would not be such a great source of inspiration as it is, and the Christian faith would not have the universal appeal that it has always had.

One of the most important factors favouring the development of the Reformation in the sixteenth and seventeenth centuries was the translation of the Bible into the vernaculars of the peoples of Europe, and the printing of those translations so that ordinary Christians could have their own copies which they could read in their own mother languages. Having read for themselves, they could then share their reinforced convictions with other people.[5] This was a new situation, very different from the Middle Ages when only the priests and monks who could read Latin had a direct access to the Bible. The ordinary Christians then had to rely on their priests for interpretation of the Biblical teaching, and on the traditions of the Church for settlement of any doctrinal controversies.[6] A situation similar to that in the Reformation occurred in the development of Christianity in Africa in the twentieth century. The translation of the Bible (or parts of it) into African languages greatly increased the possibility of the rise of 'Independent' Churches among those peoples to whom the Bible was available in their own mother tongues.[7]

This fact points to two observations which are important in our consideration of the Biblical basis for evangelization. The first concerns the contextuality of a person's response to the Gospel. Jesus was very contextual in his teaching and when a person can read the gospels for himself, he is able to have a personal encounter with Jesus Christ in a much deeper and more contextual way than when the Gospel reaches him through the preaching of other people, no matter how effective the preaching may be. Missionaries coming to Africa, especially from Protestant denominations, realized this point and were convinced of the context of the history of their own denominational background that functional literacy was an important asset in the work of evangelization. They, therefore, embarked on the teaching of functional literacy as a necessary part of their missionary enterprise on the continent.

The second point concerns the missionary demands of the Christian faith. In the New Testament, the Christian faith is called the Good News.

Good News is such that it cannot be hidden, especially when it is news about the inauguration of a new era, about the coming of better times for the people of the world. Acceptance of this Good News means that those who become committed to the Christian faith feel obliged — compelled — to share the Good News with other people. In view of this, it is no surprise, therefore, that the greatest share in the work of the evangelization of Africa was carried out by African converts among their own ethnic communities, and sometimes beyond ethnic limits when language was not a communication barrier.

Missionaries from Western world to Africa are often regarded as having made great sacrifices of their own comfort in order to bring the Christian faith to the people of Africa; but it is worthwhile to remember that African evangelists made no less sacrifices of their own comfort in missionary contribution to the establishment of Christianity in the interior of the African continent.

Evangelization — the sharing of the Good News with others — has a strong Biblical basis. This is the point to which we shall now turn, to examine more closely the nature of the Biblical call to evangelization, in the context of the Christian faith as a missionary religion.

Christianity as a Missionary Religion

To become a Christian means to decide to become a follower of Jesus of Nazareth, and to affirm him to be the Christ. But what does it mean, to follow Jesus and affirm his authority as divine? The simplest answer to this question is that to become a follower of Jesus means to become his disciple. To understand what discipleship means, we have to turn to the Bible and find out what discipleship meant among the first generation of the followers of Jesus.

The first four disciples of Jesus were fishermen; fishing along the shores of Lake Galilee was their occupation. Jesus called them from that occupation and challenged them to become 'fishers of men'. What did Jesus mean by this expression — 'fishers of men? Was he calling on these people to become cannibals? In the context of the life of Jesus with his disciples as narrated in the four Gospels, discipleship was challenged by the supporters of the then established religious institution, who brought pressure to bear upon Jesus and the disciples so that they might conform to the norms of thinking and conduct set by tradition. But Jesus and the disciples refused to be tied to the past to such an extent that tradition would become a hindrance to the development of a liberating vision of the future. To Jesus, the past was important only in as far as it formed the background for the present, but he considered it a wrong approach to remain so conditioned by the past that the future could only be seen only in terms of past glory. He had not come to destroy the past, but to fulfil it.

Discipleship among the first followers of Jesus meant proclaiming that a new era had been inaugurated, while at the same time the positive basis of the past was being strongly affirmed. It is for this reason that the teaching of the prophets had a great significance in the disciples' understanding of the Gospel. Those people who encountered Jesus and his disciples contrasted the new teaching with the prevailing religious institution, and they noticed a great difference. Their assessment of the Gospel was that there was something significantly new in the teaching of Jesus, 'and they were astonished at his teaching, for he taught as one who had authority, and not as the scribes'.

A study of the first generation of disciples is very relevant today in illuminating our understanding of the Biblical basis for evangelization. The disciples were called to be sent. And their mission was to proclaim the Good News. But what was this Good News in practical terms? We need not venture to guess an answer to this question, for Jesus answered it in his characteristically inductive way.

When John the Baptist was in prison, he sent his followers to Jesus to enquire as to whether He was the one whom John anticipated in his teaching and ministry. Jesus answered to John's messengers: 'Go and tell John what you hear and see: the blind receive their sight and the lame walk, lepers are cleansed and the deaf hear, and the dead are raised up, and the poor have good news preached to them. And blessed is he who takes no offence at me'.

Discipleship meant furthering this Good News, in its totality. It would be an unfortunate distortion of the teaching of Jesus to reduce the proclamation of the Gospel merely to preaching about the future 'Kingdom of God' in heaven, and to be concerned only with the salvation of the soul. It is clear, in both deeds and words, that Jesus was concerned with the inauguration of a new era in the totality of human experience, at both the individual and social levels. It would be a mistake also, to reduce the Gospel merely to works of social service, without affirming the theological basis of Christian action. The theological and the social dimensions of mission must be maintained in complementary relation if the biblical basis for evangelization is to determine our understanding of Christian discipleship today.

The fact that during the ministry of Jesus his disciples worked within the social context of their own ethnic community is instructive for the work of evangelization in Africa today. Christianity was introduced in the interior of Africa through the process of the modern missionary enterprise. Hardly two centuries have passed since the first pioneer missionary arrived in the interior of Africa, from Europe. The modern missionary movement coincided with the period of European colonization of non-European countries and, for a long time, mission was understood in terms of going out of one's country to spread the Christian faith abroad.

However, it is being increasingly realized that as soon as the Christian faith had been introduced by a pioneer missionary from abroad, the work of establishing Christianity in Africa was undertaken more by African evangelists than by the foreign missionaries who were strangers to the African cultural and religious background. Conditioned by their own cultural traditions and myths, the missionaries judged African cultures through the norms of their heritage. The first generation of African converts to Christianity achieved a much greater impact on their own cultures than the pioneer missionaries whose role in Africa could not be clearly distinguished by Africans from the role of colonial authorities. Thus many Africans among the first generation of converts in theory noticed no continuity between their new faith and their old culture. In practice they could understand the Christian faith only in the context of their cultural and religious experience. They, therefore, contrasted their new faith with African culture.[8]

The Nature of Christian Mission

It is necessary to clarify and qualify the terms which one uses in any discourse today. It is a mistake to assume that a word which is commonly used in a language is commonly understood in that language. An analysis of the debates and conflicts which develop in discourse can show that much confusion and obscurity prevails because there is a lack of common understanding of the basic terms commonly used by the proponents and opponents of a point of view.

One of the clearest illustrations of this observation is the controversy which developed at the end of the nineteenth century over the theory of evolution and its impact on the Christian doctrine of creation. On the one hand, some Christians felt that the theory undermined the Christian doctrine of creation. How could a person accept the theory that life evolved through a long process of natural selection in response to changing environmental conditions and at the same time believe that 'in the beginning God created' the world and everything in it? On the other hand, some natural scientists, having anchored their faith in the then apparent success of modern science, dismissed the Bible as mythical literature, unless its accounts could be authenticated by empirical research.[9]

Positivism influenced each of the two sides of the controversy to insist that its view was the authoritative one while the other was held to be mistaken. If the Christians understood the penultimate nature of the concerns and methods of science, they would not place scientific theories against the affirmations of faith. Likewise, if the scientists kept their discourse within the scope of scientific concerns and methods, they would not judge the ultimate affirmations of faith by the criteria of the provisional propositions of a scientific hypothesis. When a scientific theory is elevated to a dogma, it ceases to function as a basis for scientific investigation. And when a religious doctrine is reduced to a scientific hypothesis or a philosophical theory, it loses its value as a basis for a religious interpretation of reality.[10]

If we accept that to become a Christian means to decide to become a follower of Jesus and to affirm that he is Christ, it follows that to accept the Christian faith means to become practically committed to the full demands of Christian discipleship. To choose to become a follower of Jesus necessarily implies to become committed to the task of proclaiming the Gospel — the Good News — in its totality. Therefore, the task of evangelization cannot correctly be regarded as the specialized profession of only a few selected Christians. Every Christian, by virtue of his faith, must be involved in evangelization if he is to qualify as a follower of Jesus, according to the New Testament understanding of discipleship.

It is fortunate that ultimately it is God who judges all people, for no one is perfect and no one can claim to have achieved the great demands of discipleship which Jesus demonstrated with his life.[11] Analogically, all Christians are 'pilgrims' travelling along the difficult road of discipleship.

They can encourage each other and accompany each other in the community of faith as they carry out the task of evangelization, but no one has any biblical authority to claim more perfection in discipleship than others. 'If any one would be first, he must be last of all and servant of all'.[12]

Another insight which is significantly discernible in the Bible is that discipleship demands of each Christian to commit his whole personality to the task of proclaiming the Good News. The Christian's words must not be divorced from his conduct. It is sad and scandalous, for the Christian faith, that many Christians involved in evangelization create the impression that what they say is more important than their actions. The society to whom they proclaim the Gospel notice that the preacher's conduct is not consistent with his preaching. In such a situation, the message which the society receives is 'Do as I say, but not as I do'. But this is not the message of discipleship which Christian evangelization should proclaim. Jesus instructed his disciples as follows: 'If any man would come after me, let him deny himself and take up his cross and follow me'.[13]

A Christian who does not practise what he preaches is unlikely to be taken seriously by the society in which he proclaims the Christian faith. From the African perspective, one serious criticism of the modern missionary enterprise has been that missionaries preached the Gospel of unity but at the same time perpetuated Christian denominational rivalry. And yet, when new Churches were founded in Africa, the same missionaries accused the founders of these Churches of breaching the unity of the Church. This lack of consistency between proclamation and the application of the Christian faith in the modern missionary enterprise indicates an aspect of evangelization which needs serious attention today.[14] In his parabolical method of teaching, Jesus analogously likened proclamation without appropriate practice to salt which has lost its taste. He told his hearers: 'You are the salt of the earth; but if salt has lost its taste, how shall its saltness be restored? It is no longer good for anything except to be thrown out and trodden under foot by men'.[15]

The disciples were instructed by Jesus to be in their society as salt is to food, as light is to darkness, and as leaven is to flour in the baking process. They were instructed to practise their discipleship in such a way that they would be like the mustard seed, which is tiny but grows into a huge tree which gives a wide shade and perches many birds; like the grain seed which is sown in rich soil and produces a rich yield. Ethically, they were challenged to be like the Samaritan who felt great compassion on the person who fell victim among robbers, and helped him at his own expense until all the injuries had been healed. Spiritually, Jesus instructed his disciples to be like the 'publican' who approached God in prayer with humility, confessing that he was a sinner in great need of God's forgiveness. True repentance comes through the humble acknowledgement of our failures and weaknesses, and the affirmation of the love and power of God to forgive all those who sincerely repent. Continual repentance is a necessary ingredient of effective evangelization.

So far we have discussed the biblical basis for an individual Christian's commitment to evangelization. However, it is worthwhile and important to add that evangelization is also, and necessarily, a corporate responsibility. The Church is the community which derives its identity from its commitment to Jesus Christ. The individual Christian lives his faith within the Church and identifies himself as a Christian in the context of the Church which predates his own temporal life. The Church continues the work of evangelization after the individual has died. The Christian doctrine of the Communion of Saints is an expression of this trans-historical character of the Church.

According to the New Testament, the Church is not a building — a place of worship. Rather, it is the community which shares in fellowship the common faith in Jesus Christ.[16] The use of the term *church* to refer to a building is a late development in Church history. In the first century, there were very few or no buildings which were specifically and architecturally designed to be places of worship. Christians at the time were a persecuted minority who met in private houses, often in secret. But those communities of faith were the Church of the time. The tradition of constructing buildings specially designed for public Christian worship was not popularized until the fourth century, after the official toleration and creditation of Christianity under Constantine.

Such buildings were constructed to reflect the artistic and architectural tastes of the communities of faith who built them, in the contexts of their cultures. Hence the wide application of 'Gothic architecture' in the construction of ecclesiastical institutions during the long period of Roman influence in Europe during the Dark Ages. The Coptic and Orthodox Churches of the same periods applied other distinct forms of architecture, derived from the culture in which those Churches expressed the Christian faith.

In Africa today, many Christian congregations do not have specially designed buildings for worship. They worship in school classrooms, under trees and in open air. Many of the young Churches founded in Africa by African Christians are in this situation of having no buildings for worship and they appreciate more easily the concept of 'Church' as the community of faith, than those Churches which are directly linked to the modern Churches, which have their background in the Missionary societies from Europe and America.

There is a great tendency among African Christians to associate the concept of *Church* with the buildings which they use for worship. But it is the concept of the Church as a community which is biblical and which is of great importance in our consideration of the biblical basis for evangelization.

The Church, understood as the community whose identity is anchored in the commitment of its members to Jesus Christ, has the corporate obligation to continually implement the demands of Christian discipleship. We have observed how the Christian discipleship necessarily demands of the followers of Christ to share the 'Good News' with people who have not yet heard or accepted the Gospel of the 'Kingdom of God'. The individual Christians derive stimulation, encouragement, support and prayer for evangelization from the community of faith to which they belong.

In the gospels in the New Testament, there are accounts of how Jesus sent his disciples on missions of evangelization. Sometimes they were sent in twos, and frequently they accompanied Jesus himself in his ministry. But the objective of their task was one — to proclaim the Good News of the Kingdom of God. They often came together, under the leadership of their master, Jesus Christ, to evaluate the strengths and weaknesses of their assignments. The Church as the community charged with responsibility of continuing the work begun by Jesus Christ has the biblical mandate to follow this tradition of making continuous evaluations of Christian missionary activity in particular places and periods. This mandate was obeyed within the first generation of Christianity.

The book of the Acts of the Apostles in the New Testament is a moving record of the work of evangelization, written by someone who was himself involved in, and committed to, the work of proclaiming the Gospel in obedience to the demands of discipleship. Paul of Tarsus was a great missionary and his epistles give the Churches of today important insights into the challenges which must be faced in the task of evangelization. We need not delve into the details of elaborating those challenges here, because anyone who is interested in knowing about the missionary work of St. Paul can refer to the book of Acts of the Apostles and to his epistles in the New Testament. But we need to emphasize that evangelization, understood in the biblical perspective, is both an individual and a corporate commitment, which all Christians are instructed by Jesus Christ to pursue.

St. Paul did his missionary work as an individual with unflinching dedication and, at the same time, he wrote his many epistles as open letters to the Christian communities and individuals whom he had met, visited or hoped to visit. In those open letters he dealt suggestively with the specific challenges which he understood to be the major hindrances to effective evangelization faced by those to whom he addressed his letters.

Corporate responsibility in the work of evangelization is best illustrated in the Bible by the first recorded Ecumenical Council — the one held in Jerusalem and given documentation in the Acts, chapter 15, and also in Galatians, chapters 2 and 3. In the first Council of Jerusalem, there was rigorous debating among the missionary leaders of the time. The pressing common issue which was challenging all the Churches in the Graeco-Roman world at the time, and which was thoroughly discussed in that Council, was the question of the relationship between culture and the Christian faith. The leaders of the Church felt it necessary to reach a general agreement or policy regarding the attitude which the Church should adopt in the contexts of Judaism and Graeco-Roman cultural traditions. After debating and presenting various points of view, the agreed principle resulting from that Council remains instructive for Christian evangelization today.

It was agreed that the cultural background of a prospective convert to Christianity was of peripheral significance as far as his commitment to the Christian faith was concerned.[17] What was of primary importance was that the convert affirmed the lordship and the divinity of Jesus Christ, and that he was committed to subjecting his future life to this new faith. The Christian community would provide the fellowship in which he would grow to concretize his new commitment. Questions of conduct and attitude in relation to his culture and religious background would be solved through criteria determined by the practical implications of the new faith which he had chosen to accept. The cultural and religious background would not determine the faith, since that was given in the Gospel. But the life of the convert would be fulfilled, or made more worthwhile, without denying his cultural and religious background.

Following this principle, the Church made a great and irreversible impact on Graeco-Roman religion and culture. To this point, we shall briefly turn and elaborate on the distinction between evangelization and proselytization.

Evangelization and Making Proselytes

We have seen that evangelization as portrayed in the New Testament involves faith and practice, and that proclamation of the Christian faith without living according to the demands of the proclamation, is an approach which falls far short of the meaning of Christian discipleship as Jesus meant it to be for his disciples. But what does it mean to live according to the Christian faith and proclaim the Gospel following the model which Jesus set for his disciples?

Many answers to this question are possible, and the existence of numerous Christian denominations today — each claiming to follow faithfully the model of Jesus — is indicative of the very wide variety of answers which have been worked out. It is theologically honest to admit that none of those answers is a perfect reproduction of the model of Jesus.

Every Christian who would accept the New Testament meaning of discipleship which we have elaborated would agree also that a faithful follower of Jesus Christ is necessarily challenged by his commitment to share his faith with other people. But the question remains as to how he should guide those whom he converts to the Christian faith, to express that faith and relate it to their cultural and religious heritage. He himself, as the evangelizer, may have worked out his own synthesis between the Gospel and his background, but it does not follow that his synthesis is necessarily applicable to those whom he converts. This question has been a great missionary problem since the first century of Christianity. The first Council of Jerusalem considered it a sufficiently significant problem to deserve an ecumenical solution.

One basic problem among the first generation of Christians was that there seemed to be no clear distinction between Judaism and the Christian faith. There were both Jews and non-Jews within the Christian community. Before John the Baptist and Jesus Christ began their ministry, there was in the Graeco-Roman world the practice of proselytization which the Jews had designed for recruiting non-Jews into Judaism. Non-Jews who felt attracted to the Hebrew religious heritage were allowed to become proselytized into Judaism, provided that they willingly agreed to undergo circumcision, which was regarded as the most significant cultural practice distinguishing the widely dispersed Hebrew community from all the other peoples of the Graeco-Roman world. Circumcision among the Hebrews was considered so important that no one could be accepted as a proselyte into Judaism without undergoing this ritual, which every Jewish male child underwent on the eighth day of life.

However, the fact remained that circumcision would not change a non-Jew into a Jew any more than the acculturation of an African into European culture can change him into a European. So a proselyte, even after undergoing the ritual of circumcision, would not be accepted as a full member of the synagogue, and in the temple at Jerusalem there was a court specially reserved for Gentiles. This reservation was extended to all Gentile proselytes, no matter how thoroughly they might have studied the Law and the Prophets of the Hebrew religious tradition.

Among the first generation of Christians, there were those who believed that since Christianity had originated within the Hebrew religious heritage, non-Jews who chose to follow the Christian faith must undergo the ritual of circumcision, as had been the case with all those who wanted to be proselytized into Judaism. Other Christians, including St. Paul, believed that Jesus had inaugurated a completely new sense of community, which was based not on cultural identity but on faith in God through Jesus Christ. This latter view prevailed at the first Ecumenical Council of Jerusalem, which agreed with St. Paul that in Jesus Christ there is neither Jew nor Gentile, neither slave nor master, neither male nor female — all are one in Jesus Christ. All that was necessary for admission into the Christian 'Way' was faith in Jesus Christ. Other considerations were of peripheral significance. With this principle Christianity became a universally open religious movement which people of any culture could join without prejudice or discrimination, and in principle the Christian faith has so remained ever since.

The demand that non-Jews should be circumcised in order to be accepted as proselytes into Judaism was a requirement that non-Jews be first acculturated into the Hebrew culture before they could be accepted as partakers of the Hebrew religious heritage. The winning of converts into Christianity after the first Council of Jerusalem was based on a very different criterion. The admission of converts into the Christian faith would not depend on acculturation into any culture. Rather, the converts were confirmed to become full members of the Church once they had decided to become followers of Jesus and affirmed the basic beliefs of the Christian community.

The Modern Missionary Movement of the nineteenth and twentieth centuries through which Christianity was introduced to the interior of Africa ignored the basic missionary principle endorsed by the first Council of Jerusalem, in spite of the fact that most missionaries were very piously committed to a literal interpretation of the Bible. In principle, the missionary societies which comprised the Modern Missionary Movement reverted to the pre-conciliar demand of acculturation as the precondition which prospective African converts must fulfil before they could be accepted as Christians. The cultural heritage of the various denominations took the view Judaism had taken before the first Council of Jerusalem. Most missionaries demanded that African converts must abandon their African culture and religion totally, and imitate the cultures of the pioneer missionaries before they could be admitted into the Church. This was a proselytizing approach of making Christian converts and it made the African understanding of Christianity rather superficial.

The superficiality of African Christianity during the pioneer period of modern missionary activity in the interior of Africa lay in the fact that African converts undertook the Christian faith merely in terms of denouncing their traditional cultures and religious beliefs, and adopting the new cultural norms which the missionaries had introduced.[18] Literacy was a very new and exciting cultural innovation which was associated with missionary activity, and so among many African peoples, becoming a Christian was considered equivalent to acquiring the skills of literacy;[19] becoming a fully credited member of the denomination which the missionary wanted to expand in his mission activity. This led to denominational competition to win as many African converts as possible in order to swell the numerical strength of the denomination. African converts did not understand the historical roots of western denomi-nationalism, but in choosing to become Christians, they realized that they were not only detached from their cultural and religious roots but that at the same time African converts from one area could be divided into followers of several denominations which were in open competition and rivalry.

The remark that the African understanding of Christianity was rather superficial does not mean that African converts were not genuine in their faith. Rather, it explains why African Christians found it difficult to argue out a rationale in support of Christianity in response to African criticisms of the Christian faith as it was presented by the Modern Missionary Enterprise. Articulations for the defence of Christianity against African criticism were for many decades the monopoly of missionaries. The quest for African Christian theology was not sounded until the second half of the twentieth century. But even then, the call was sounded to a large extent by missionaries who felt that Christianity as a world religion would be lacking in an important respect if African Christians did not share with the rest of the universal Church their understanding of the Gospel. One of the first missionaries to express this anticipation of the African contribution to the world Church was John V. Taylor as he was concluding his study entitled *The Growth of the Church in Buganda.*[20]

The superficiality in the African understanding of Christianity thrived for a long time because African converts to the Christian faith had adopted the presupposition, held by many missionaries, that Africans were incapable of articulating, in a sophisticated way, their understanding of theology and philosophy, and that missionaries could act as spokesmen for Africans in theological and philosophical matters. This presupposition generated a great inconsistency between the theoretical framework on which Africans did evangelization and the practical implementation of the 'great commission' to 'go into all the world and preach the Gospel'.

The Modern Missionary Enterprise introduced Christianity in Africa as an integral part of European culture. Many African Christians understood it as such. Later, when in anti-colonial movements Africans launched attacks on European power and culture, the missionary enterprise was not spared the shock. The refutation of the view that Christianity could not be understood apart from the western culture is one of the factors underlying the establishment of Independent Churches during the colonial period. Some African Christians realized that the various denominational interpretations of the Christian faith were not the only possible interpretations. It may be argued that the failure of the Modern Missionary Enterprise to adhere to the theological principle endorsed by the first Ecumenical Council of Jerusalem did not justify Africans to found their own Churches. However, the question of justification and blame is beside the point we have reached in this discussion of distinction between evangelization and proselytization. What is more important for our understanding of the biblical basis for evangelization today is to learn from the mistakes of the past in order to improve in the future. The Modern Missionary Enterprise saw a great achievement in making Christianity a world-wide religion with adherents in every continent. But it had its shortcomings, especially in failing to heed the theological insight derived from the Council of Jerusalem with regard to the relationship between the Christian faith and culture.

Evangelization must be distinguished from proselytization if its biblical basis is to be the criterion determining the proclamation of the Gospel today. If it is to remain within the teaching of Jesus today, evangelization must help the people of every culture to fulfil their ultimate aspirations of cultural and religious heritage. This cannot be done if proselytization is substituted for evangelization, for proselytization will produce converts who are not free to respond, authentically and directly, to the promise of the Good News of the 'Kingdom of God'. One illustration of the distinction between evangelization and proselytization is the analogy which follows.

The world in which we live is like a dark cave in which all the races of mankind find themselves trapped. Everyone in the cave believes and hopes that there must be a loose piece of rock somewhere along the walls of the dark cave, and that outside there is bright sunshine and more freedom. If only a small piece of rock would fall out of the cave wall, then mankind would realize a long-awaited aspiration. Everyone continues groping along the walls and hoping for a better future. Then suddenly, by chance or through providence, someone touches somewhere along one of the walls and a piece of rock falls down to the floor of the cave and beams of sunlight flood the whole cave. With that aspiration fulfilled, the people rush towards the little hole, wanting to get out of the cave and run to freedom. But the person who touched the piece of rock that fell and brought in light blocks the way, insisting that he must lead and become the master of all the cave-dwellers because he is the one who brought light to them. The cave-dwellers refuse this self-imposed responsibility and shout that they can find the way to freedom and light without the aid of leadership of the one who claims to have brought the light. Instead they advise him that he is no different from the rest and so they all should co-operate in order to make a bigger hole in the cave wall so that everyone might get out without competition. Some even suggest that, if everyone joined efforts, they might demolish the cave altogether and attain happiness and freedom once and for all. But the self-appointed 'master' still blocks the way because he is convinced that he must lead and be acknowledged as the leader. So there continues to be tensions in the cave.

According to the biblical view as we have discussed it, evangelization is like a pilgrimage in which all Christians are involved. The more people join the pilgrimage, the happier the corporate journey. But no one along the way is greater than the other, since the destination is set by God, and the call to this pilgrimage is inspired by the One who, though once a human being, is the Son of God who has gone the whole journey before these pilgrims who are following his footsteps towards the 'Kingdom of God'. According to this analogy, the great commitment on the part of the pilgrims tells the whole world of the greatness of the destination, and of the joy that fills all those who join in the journey, in spite of its hardships.

NOTES

1. For a sympathetic study of these religions see Ninian Smart, *The Religious Experience of Mankind,* London/Glasgow; Collins/Fontana, 1971.

2. The Common Bible contains all the canonical books accepted in the main confessional families of Christianity. Its publication has been a great ecumenical achievement.

3. For a complementary presentation of both Testaments, see William Neil's *One Volume Bible Commentary,* London: Hodder and Stoughton, 1962; G. Ernest Wright and Reginald Fuller, *The Book of the Acts of God,* Penguin Books, 1965.

4. The History of English Versions of the Bible is presented in *The Oxford Annotated Bible,* eds. Herbert G. May and Bruce M. Metzger, New York: Oxford University Press, 1962, (RSV), pp. 1551–75.

5. Philip Hughes, *A Popular History of the Reformation,* New York: Image Books/- Doubleday, 1960, pp. 191–98.

6. *Op.Cit.,* pp. 24–30.

7. This point has been emphasized by David B. Barrett in his *Schism and Renewal in Africa,* London: Oxford University Press, 1968. Also J.S. Mbiti, *Bible and Theology in African Christianity, op.cit.,* pp. 22–45.

8. Herbert J. Muller emphasized that "no religion that succeeds can be wholly new. Although it must appear to improve upon the past, it cannot break with the past; it must satisfy hopes and desires conditioned by the past; and as it takes root, it draws still more from the past". *The Use of the Past,* New York: Oxford University Press, 1952, p. 191. The Christian faith is initially accepted as a new way of life discontinuous with the past, but as it becomes established and rooted, its indebtedness to the receiving culture is increasingly appreciated. That is the situation in African Christianity as it enters the 21st century.

9. On the controversy over the Theory of Evolution, see E.O. James, *Christianity and other Faiths,* London: Hodder and Stoughton, 1968; William Irvine, *Apes, Angels and Victorians: A Joint Biography of Darwin and Huxley,* London: Weidenfeld and Nicolson, 1956.

10. This point is lucidly elaborated by John Polkinghorne, *One World: The Interaction of Science and Theology,* Princeton, New Jersey: Princeton University Press, 1986; Roger Pilkington, *World Without End,* London/Glasgow: Collins/Fontana, 1961.

11. Mark 10: 17–22.

12. Mark 9: 33–37.

13. Mark 8: 34–9:1; James 1: 22–25.

14. Erasto Muga, *African Response to Western Christian Religion,* Nairobi: E.A. Literature Bureau, 1975, pp. 116–182.

15. Matthew 5:13.

16. H.A. Guy, *The Church in the New Testament,* London: Macmillan, 1969: V.L. Gingrich, *The Church,* Kisumu, Kenya: Evangel, 1970

17. For a critical discussion of the Council of Jerusalem in relation to the Missionary enterprise in E. Africa, see J.N.K. Mugambi, "Some Perspectives of Christianity in the Context of the Modern Missionary Enterprise in E. Africa with special Reference to Kenya", *African Christian Theology,* Nairobi: Heinemann, 1989.

18. J.V. Taylor, *The Primal Vision,* London: SCM Press, 1963, ch. 1.

19. W.B. Anderson, *The Church in East Africa 1840-1974,* Dodoma: Central Tanganyika Press, 1977, pp. 111-117.

20. J.V. Taylor, *The Growth of the Church in Buganda,* London: SCM Press, 1958.

Chapter Two

CHRISTIAN THEOLOGY
AS CONTEXTUAL RESPONSE

How local should one go in emphasizing the contextual nature of Christian theological reflection? One way of answering this question is by affirming that in the modern world, the smallest viable socio-political unit is the modern nation and that, therefore, Christians ought to define their identity in terms of their national belonging. However, within the nation, the question of the meaning of a 'local Church' still arises. What is a local Church? Is it at the level of the congregation (weekly liturgical fellowship), of the parish (a collection of geographically close liturgical communities conveniently grouped together), of the diocese (a collection of adjacent parishes grouped together for the purpose of convenient ecclesial administration), or of a nation (in which there are many Christian denominations each with its own ecclesial persuasions)? Again, this difficult question might be answered by emphasizing that the Church ought to define its locality in terms of the national identities in which it is established. Such an answer would appear to be appropriate in the context of the development of modern nationalism in every part of the world.

However, within the nation, there are particularities of congregations, parishes and dioceses in any one denomination. There are also varying perspectives of the Church's mission and theology, from one denomination to another. May these particularities be overlooked in the quest for a viable and consistent definition of a local Church?

The richness of Christian theological development will depend greatly on the degree of readiness, among Church leaders and theologians, to welcome and take seriously the particularities of context within a nation as significant factors contributing to the total mosaic of the universal Christian experience and expression. At the global level, the positive impact of Christianity as a universal faith relevant for all humanity will be assessed more effectively if the national and regional particularities are acknowledged and appreciated. This attitude of listening to and encouraging each other has already become a positive aspect of the Modern Ecumenical Movement, even though it is often easier to *acknowledge* the diverse particularities than to appreciate the difficulties which confront people in situations different from our own. It was this realization of the human failure to appreciate the suffering of others that moved the black slaves in North America to sing, under the yoke of their white master, the moving spiritual, 'Nobody knows the trouble I've seen'. This realization and its literary expression has its parallel today, and it would be a great pity if the Church as a social institution, as the herald of a more humane society on earth in anticipation of the Kingdom of God, were to plunge itself consciously in such failure. It would be a great pity if, within the Christian community, some members were compelled by others to sing, with the slaves who composed the spiritual, 'Nobody knows the trouble I've seen'.[1]

The question of readiness to take seriously the problems of others, especially when we are at least partly responsible for causing them, leads to a further point which is worth considering — the apparent tension between the principles of universality and particularity in Christian theological experience and expression.

It is a great theological blunder to dogmatically universalize religious (or other) views which are produced and developed in one particular existential situation. Why should the norms codified in a particular culture and situation be dogmatically imposed upon the rest of the world? If 'to err is human', how does a person (or group) justify himself and others in support of his view that he has arrived at an infallible truth which is relevant and applicable both to himself and to the rest of humanity? Moreover, what justification does he have for imposing his views upon other people, especially when what is at stake is religious truth?

The argument of self-justification among some Christian missionaries during the colonial period was that African peoples were like children who could not understand or express themselves, and that the missionary must, therefore, appoint himself to the task of telling them who and what they really were, and what they lacked. The African was then expected to bow with gratitude to the apparently benevolent interpreter and say: 'You understand us: you know us completely: you "know" in the way we "know".'[2] Again, this attitude has its parallels today, and African Christian theologians outrightly reject what Professor J.S. Mbiti refers to as "theological engineering" and defines as:

> The process by which expatriate and overseas Christians are dictating to African Christians the kind of theology they should evolve in their own house.[3]

If the Church is the universal community of people who share a common faith in Jesus Christ as the Son of God and Saviour of Mankind, then its members are compelled by their common faith to learn from one another in brotherhood and sincerity, without the attitude of domination and without a superiority complex on the part of, say, a section of that universal Christian community. The enhancement of such mutual understanding and enrichment is, and should be, a great priority on the agenda of the modern ecumenical movement.

On the other hand, it is also erroneous to impose on others a dogmatically particularized universalist view. Such an imposition becomes an insult to the religious sensibility of those who do not recognize that view as universally meaningful or particularly relevant in their own existential situation. How does one arrive at a universalist view? On what basis does a person (or group) decide that a view, which he considers to be universal in relevance and applicability, would be appreciated as such by those others to whom it is offered as a solution to their ultimate questions?

Karl Barth appealed to Revelation as the ultimate source of knowledge about the nature of man and of the human predicament; but even in his theology, the notion of objectivity is not recognized as having any relevance to man's apprehension of God's universal revelation. According to Barth, God as the ultimate and infinite Reality reveals himself to humanity; but man can only respond in his finitude, subjectively, to that unconditional self-disclosure of the wholly other. As Colin Brown has observed,

> Barth sees God as utterly transcendent. He is not to be identified directly with anything in the world, not even the words of Scripture. Revelation comes to men in the same way as a vertical line intersects a horizontal plane, or as a tangent touches a circle. Because it is contact with the Wholly Other we cannot even describe it. All we can do (and all that the biblical writers can do) is to describe what they felt like after it.[4]

Jesus was fully aware of the problems of particularizing universalist principles and imposing their practical application on each and every existential situation. Such was the proscriptive approach of Rabbinical Judaism against which Jesus was frequently critical because of its absurd legalism. Instead, Jesus commended an inductive approach in which his hearers were challenged to discern the practical implications of universally relevant principles, according to the situational ethical demand of 'Love your neighbour as yourself'.

When Jesus was asked to comment on the greatest commandment, he made no abstract elaboration. The questioner knew what that commandment stated — Love God with your whole self and your neighbour as yourself — and so there was no need to add further universal, general abstractions. But the questioner's difficulty lay in determining the practical application of this universal principle. So he asked Jesus to explain: 'But who is my neighbour?' Jesus could have answered him by entering into an elaborate, philosophical abstraction as a definition of 'my neighbour'. But instead of beginning his answer with words such as: 'My neighbour is. . .', he narrated a parable — 'A man was going down from Jerusalem to Jericho. . .' After narrating the parable, he bounced the original question back to his questioner: 'Which of these three (the priest, the Levite and the Samaritan), do you think, proved neighbour to the man who fell among the robbers?' The questioner, considering the context of the parable, was left in no doubt with regard to the question 'Who is my neighbour?' (Luke 10:25–37). The conclusion of Jesus in that discussion was not 'That is my neighbour!' Rather, he issued a practical challenge to his questioner — 'Go and do likewise!' The questioner (like all of us in human society) was left to accept and apply the challenge in similar situations, or to reject it.

Paul in his letters to various Churches and individuals was also aware of this difficulty of particularizing universal principles, and took care to differentiate between what he considered to be the universal tenets of the Christian faith, and the commendable practical applications of such tenets in particular existential situations. Hence his many letters in response to the particular challenges which each of the addressed communities of faith and of individuals was facing in living and expressing the new faith within their existential contexts. To some Churches such as Corinth, and Thessalonica, and to some individuals such as Timothy, Paul even found it necessary to write two letters, the second of which was meant to reiterate some of the points he had made in his earlier letter, and also deal with issues which he had not explained in the first set of epistles.

Furthermore, Paul was particular in differentiating between his own personal opinion on the one hand and the basic Christian teaching as he understood it, on the other. He made such a distinction, for instance, when he was responding to the moral problems of marriage as experienced in the Corinthian Church of his time. In making this distinction he gave allowance of the possibility that on matters to which he had expressed his own opinion, other Christians might deal with the same problem differently, without necessarily contravening the essential and universal proclamation of the Christian faith: 'Now concerning the unmarried, I have no command of the Lord, but I have my opinion as one who by the Lord's mercy is trusthworthy.' (1 Cor. 7:25).

Such modesty in matters of religious opinion is worthy of commendation, and it is in support of this unrestrictive approach that Jesus left his hearers (and ourselves) free to decide whether or not to follow the practical implications of his teaching, which is in accordance with the 'Kingdom of God' he introduced to mankind. Thus freedom of decision and action are central affirmations for Christians in applying the practical implications of the Gospel in particular existential situations.

Philosophically, the problem inherent in applying the two apparently contradictory principles of universalization and particularization may be explained as an indication of that endless conflict between deductive and inductive reasoning. In deductive reasoning one begins with a universal proposition as a major premise of argumentation, and judges particular cases on the basis of that major premise. Within syllogistic logic, this form of reasoning is taken for granted, and the conclusion of the argument is determined negatively, affirmatively or neutrally, depending on whether the minor proposition is within or without the major terms which are predicated in the major premise. For illustration, note the following deductive argument:

All people are sinners;
I am a person,
Therefore I am a sinner.

This argument is logical in the sense that the conclusion is consistently derived from the major and minor propositions.

Deductive logic is not ultimately concerned with truth. Rather, it is concerned with the consistency of argumentation, in accordance with the rules of deductive reasoning. If the major premise is false, the conclusion will also be false, even though the argument may be logically consistent. The question as to how one establishes the truth or falsity of universal propositions, which in turn determine the truth or falsity of conclusions in deductive logic, is outside the scope of deductive reasoning. The question of truth and falsity is an epistemological one. Therefore, if in our illustration it were not true that all people are sinners, it would also be untrue that I am a sinner. Moreover, in deductive argumentation, it is assumed that the meaning of all the terms involved is known and remains constant throughout the argument, so that in our illustration the term 'sinner' retains the same meaning in both the major proposition and the conclusion.

It is worthwhile to discuss this illustration a little further to indicate the problem inherent in the task of establishing truth where deductive reasoning is involved.

The view that 'all people are sinners' has been an issue of philosophical debate and theological reflection for a long time in the Western intellectual tradition, and may be a point of chasmic difference between traditional Western Christian theology and the traditional African view of human nature. Whereas the Catholic Christian tradition has maintained the doctrine of 'original sin' and considered man as a 'fallen creature' who could be redeemed only by the grace of God, through divine forgiveness, Jean Jacques Rousseau maintained that man is ultimately 'good', and is corrupted only by the society in which he is brought up. The traditional African view of human nature is that man is ultimately 'good', but unlike Rousseau's view of society as the basic corrupting influence of the human individual, African religious thought explains the origin of evil in terms of agents other than human (such as animals — hyena, hare, chameleon, etc.) who originally corrupted God's message to humanity, that man would live without suffering, immortally.

The agent who delivered the message of immortality from God to man is believed to have distorted it in transit, so that when it reached man, it was contrary to what God had decided to be the eternal human nature. But since God never alters his word, the predicament of suffering and mortality remained the nature of man. And so it remains. But in the African view, man is not ultimately alienated from God, otherwise he would not exist in the African ontological system in which various ontological categories (including God) exist in a balance of interrelationships that must not be upset at any point.

These three views could each be a major premise in a deductive argument. Which of them is correct and which are wrong? This question cannot be objectively answered, so the question of how to establish truth and falsity remains puzzling. The truth of universal propositions in deductive reasoning remains unconfirmed, no matter how logically consistent deductive syllogisms might be. It is at this point that Christian theology turns to Revelation to confirm its universal affirmations. Nevertheless, as we have seen, revelation remains a subjective criterion and only.those who can confirm the affirmations of revelation in their own experience can accept it as true. Others may dismiss it as irrational jargon.

How does one respond when two contradictory affirmations are attributed to the same source of Revelation as, for example, the doctrines of Predestination and Free Will in Christian theology? Is man absolutely free, or absolutely determined by the power of God? There are differences of opinion on this question in Christian theology. Therefore, one cannot establish a conclusive justification for imposing one's own religious view on other people, even when one uses deductive reasoning in support of one's religious conviction. The best that such a person can do to win others to his religious disposition, is to describe (or 'confess', to use a more familiar Christian theological term) his own religious orientation to others, and commend it to them in the hope that they too will find it satisfying in their own religious quest.

In inductive reasoning, one establishes universal principles by empirically observing regularity in the behaviour (or inner character) of something, and relating this behaviour to previously observed cases. Then one formulates generalizations, assuming that other cases in future will follow the same universal principles which one has formulated or assumed on the basis of such previous observations. The basic problem of inductive reasoning is that it is impossible to observe all cases in order to draw up a universal principle with the certainty that all particularities have been taken into consideration in the principle which is formulated to cover all cases. If it were possible to enumerate all cases and observe them, the formulation of a universal principle by the inductive method might then be unnecessary, because such inductively drawn up principles are formulated as guidelines to determine the general character of things within the universe without having to enumerate and scrutinize all cases. In view of this impossibility, therefore, one can only observe some cases or some aspects of the universal phenomena under consideration.

For instance, previous experience has confirmed, to man's thinking, the regularity of sunshine, sunset and the seasons. Man accepts this regularity even though his life is only a tiny fraction of the whole history of the universe. On this basis, those who live within the tropics have come to believe that without fail the sun will rise tomorrow morning at almost the same time as it did this morning and yesterday morning, while those outside the tropics believe that summer and winter will come at certain particular periods in any one year.

Those who live outside the tropics also know, through accumulated experience, that some days in the year are longer than others, according to the seasons. The irregularity of the length of days and nights is not so obvious to people living near the Equator, and many Africans from tropical Africa do not realize the impact of such differences until they visit Europe and North America where the cycle of four seasons in a year is obvious to someone living there.

The solar system seems so regular that one would be greatly shocked if the sun did not rise one day, or if it rose from the west rather than from the east. Logically, however, the fact that the sun has regularly risen every day for millions of days is not sufficient reason to make one suppose that it will rise 'as usual', tomorrow or next year. Yet we do not normally doubt the regularity of the solar system, so we plan our activities ahead of time.

It is a matter of 'common sense', that we take this regularity for granted. Even African peoples who, according to Professor Mbiti, do not conceive of the future 'beyond a few months from now', plant crops to forestall famine, and bring up their children in anticipation of the time when the children will grow old and become elders in the community — a preparation that lasts a whole generation. If the regularity of the solar system were not taken for granted, such plans would be impossible to implement. Modern science, on the basis of the theory of probability, has invented mathematical models which form grounds for relative certainty. The greater the probability, the greater the degree of certainty. However, religious faith operates on the basis of absolute certainty, not mathematically calculated ratios of probability, even though such ratios may reinforce religious beliefs. The problem with which we are concerned here is how a religious person arrives at such absolute certainty. Inductive reasoning does not provide conclusive grounds for such absoluteness.

For illustration, it is worthwhile to examine how inductive reasoning arrives at its conclusions. We may take the same example of the solar system. The inductive basis of the belief that the sun will rise tomorrow runs as follows:

> For millions of days the sun has risen every morning regularly;
> This morning the sun rose as usual:
> Therefore, tomorrow the sun will rise in the morning as usual.

Of course, the modern educated person does not normally phrase his argument like this when he is entering appointments in his diary. That the sun will rise tomorrow, next week, next year and always, is so obvious to him that he takes that regularity for granted, as a matter of common sense.

Like deductive argumentation, inductive reasoning is very vulnerable as far as the truth of its conclusions is concerned. The conclusion continues to be assumed on the basis of past observation, until it is contradicted by new, contrary experience. The basic problem is that one cannot be absolutely certain that the principle on which the conclusion about future cases is reached will be operative in the future. In the case of our illustration, for example, we may agree with Bertrand Russell, that we have a firm belief that the sun will rise in the future because it has risen in the past. If we are challenged as to why we believe that it will continue to rise as heretofore, we may appeal to the laws of motion: the earth, we shall say, is a freely rotating body, and such bodies do not cease to rotate unless something interferes from outside, and there is nothing to interfere with the earth between now and tomorrow. Of course, it might be doubted whether we are quite certain that there is nothing outside to interfere, but this is not the interesting doubt. The interesting doubt is as to whether the laws of motion will remain in operation until tomorrow. If this doubt is raised, we find ourselves in the same position as when the doubt about the sunrise was first raised.[5]

We need only recall the great resistance with which new scientific observations were greeted in Europe, to realize the immensity of the disturbance which may result from new, unexpected inductive experience which contradicts knowledge that is taken for granted. Until the middle of the seventeenth century, Western experts in human anatomy believed that blood circulated through the body like a 'smooth stream' which never stopped flowing until death. When William Harvey published his book announcing his discovery that the heart functioned like a pump which distributed blood throughout the body, the announcement was greeted with contempt by the experts of that time. 'Whoever heard of the heart beating like a pump?', they asked. Today we take this discovery to be common knowledge, and no one who has been exposed to modern biological education would consider this as new information, not even a primary-school child.[6]

When Galilei Galileo and Copernicus challenged Ptolemaic cosmology, they were tortured to force them to recant their discovery that it was the sun, not the earth, that was the centre of this universe, and that it was the earth that revolved round the sun rather than vice versa. Today that discovery is taken as common knowledge among those who are exposed to modern education about the solar system. A third illustration is that of Charles Darwin's Theory of Evolution. When he published it, many people, especially uncritical Christians, thought that he was totally wrong. Did the Bible not state that 'In the beginning, God created man?' Who then was Darwin to challenge the Bible which was the word of God? Today the theory of evolution is taken for granted by most people, including Christians, and the mutation of species is no longer a strange notion in the modern understanding of biology.[7]

In considering inductive reasoning within the religious demension of human life, it is clear that this approach is also used as a means to persuade people to follow or accept a particular religious orientation or practice. Consider the following advertisement, for example:

> Millions are going. Will you be there? You are cordially invited to the memorial of Jesus Christ's death — Thursday March 23, after sunset — At All Kingdom Halls of Jehova's Witnesses. Seats Free. No Collection.[8]

The appeal of this advertisement is based on the expectation that since millions of people have attended such a function in the past and would be attending the 1978 repetition of the function, the reader would feel persuaded also to join the 'millions' on the advertised occasion. According to the advertisement, 'In 1977, 5,107,518 people were present for this important occasion. Jesus Christ himself instituted a memorial of his death on the night before he died. . . .'

We need not delve into a discussion of the theological accuracy of the message carried in this advertisement. But it is cited here to indicate that the inductive approach can also lead to a misunderstanding of the essence of Christianity (or of any other religion). That advertisement gives the impression that Jesus Christ's death is just like any other human death, and the doctrine of the Resurrection which is basic to the Christian faith does not feature at all. 'What is so special about the "memorial"?', a non-Christian reading that advertisement might ask. And from the words of the advertisement, he would not get any convincing answer, except the announcement that 'millions are going'. So the problem of establishing the validity of religious truth on the basis of inductive reasoning remains unresolved.

The foregoing digression into a discussion of deductive and inductive reasoning is not meant to distract attention from our consideration of universalization and particularization as principles for guiding Christian theological reflection on missionary activity. Rather, the discussion has helped in indicating a fundamental problem to be resolved when one tries to establish grounds for preferring the one approach to the other. Furthermore, it has been shown in the discussion that neither the deductive approach nor the inductive one provides an absolute theological justification for imposing one's religious views on other people, or for insisting that one is right in religious matters while other people are absolutely wrong.

This insight is very important, especially today in the Ecumenical Movement, when Christians have to discern the practical implications of their Christian commitment to the Christian faith with regard to many complex issues that characterize our contemporary world. Depending on which of the two theological approaches a Christian theologian bases his reflection, there is always the temptation for the Christian to insist that his theological position over a particular secular issue is the only valid interpretation, and that all others are wrong (or theologically unsound).

In view of the foregoing discussion, it is worth remembering that the theological position for which a Christian opts in a contextual response, is greatly influenced by his own religious background, cultural heritage, and also by the practical demands of the particular existential situation in which he has to live. It is for this reason that the theological approaches of Jesus and Paul with regard to the secular issues of their time, as discussed earlier, would be instructive for contemporary Christianity, in emphasizing the necessity to respect and appreciate other people's interpretations, even when we may not agree with them.

Most Christian theists resolve the problem by interpreting the Bible as God's revelation to man; but there are differences among themselves when they work out what 'revelation' implies. To some, saying that 'the Bible is the Word of God' is taken to mean that God has literally 'spoken' in the Bible and that, therefore, the words recorded in that book must be accepted and acted upon at their face value. According to this literal understanding of inspiration, the Bible is like an instructor's manual which must be consulted whenever the believer encounters any problem in actual life, just as one would consult the manufacturer's manual whenever a difficulty arises in operating a machine that one had newly purchased.

One of the most disturbing shortcomings of this approach is that when some problems are encountered which happen not to have been specifically covered in the 'manual' (for example drug addiction, abortion, smoking, fashion, popular dancing, the use of violence and the like), those who hold this interpretation peruse desperately through the Bible's pages, looking for a verse to quote as a source of direction for the appropriate course of action or thinking to take. Unfortunately, such quotations are often made out of their contexts, without appreciating the whole message of the passages in which they occur. This has been done, for example, in support of glossolalia —

speaking in tongues. Those to whom this view of the Bible appeals would find it difficult to accept the theory of evolution (and some other modern scientific ideas), because it seems to them to contradict the infallible Biblical statement that God created the world, including man and all other living things, in six days and then he rested on the seventh.

To other Christians, the statement that the Bible is God's Word is interpreted to mean that this book contains a record of certain people's encounter with God, and that this record, taken as a whole, provides to the others a clue to a particular religious view of human relationship, between man and man, and between man and God. The Biblical message, according to this view, cannot be discerned by merely turning to any specific verse in the Bible and quoting it in the same way as one would refer to a paragraph in an instructor's or manufacturer's manual. Rather, the Bible is accepted in its wholeness, as a library, not as a novel, poem, history textbook, scientific thesis or dreamer's fantasy. It is considered a composite book which, within its covers, contains history, law, poetry, fiction, prophecy, mystical experience, arithmetical calculations, prayers and other forms of literary expression. Within this library, certain dominant themes run through every one of its books, to give it a unity which makes the Bible a very useful book for those who would take the trouble to study it and apply the insights, which they might derive from it, to their practical living in relations with other people and also with God (for those who believe in him).

This view of the Bible cannot be rightly deemed to be less Christian merely because of its rejection of superficial literal interpretation of the Biblical message. Its followers are, I think, more appreciative of the richness of the literary quality of this basic Christian book, and of its richness as a source to illuminate the religious dimension of human life.

Christians who hold either of these two views of the Bible accept it as the record of God's revelation to man. However, as we have seen, there are differences of opinion in expressing what this means. Earlier on in our discussion, we alluded to Karl Barth's understanding of Revelation. It is worthwhile to turn to him again to consider his view of the Christian Scriptures — the Bible. In the words of Colin Brown, we may follow Barth's theology from where we stopped: In his dialectical phase, Barth had compared the Word with a tangent touching a circle and a line intersecting a plane. But just as a line may be defined as length without breadth, so Barth's doctrine of the Word seemed to be encountered without content. For the God who revealed himself is not an object of time and space. He is one who is Wholly Other, and therefore, strictly speaking, indescribable. And if this is really the case, there is nothing more to be said. But in the *Church Dogmatics* Barth has clarified satisfaction . . . Here he speaks of the threefold form of the Word of God: Christ, Scripture and proclamation.[9]

These three aspects of the Word of God have their encounter with man in history. So Barth's dialectical distinction between God and man, eternity and history, is brought within the scope of man's faith in God; within man's end of that dialectical tension. Without entering into lengthy discussion of Barth's dogmatic theology, it is worthwhile to consider briefly the interpretation of his contemporary theologian — Rudolf Bultmann — who held a view of the Christian Scriptures that was diametrically opposed to Barth's. According to Bultmann, 'the historical person of Jesus was very soon turned into a myth in primitive Christianity.'

John Macquarrie, commenting on Bultmann's theological project of demythologization, has made the following observation:

> It is this myth which now confronts us in the New Testament, and it is impossible to get behind it to the historical Jesus. The historical facts whatever they may have been, have undergone irreversible metamorphosis into the story of a divine pre-existent being who became incarnate and atoned by his blood for the sins of men, rose from the dead, ascended into heaven and would, as was believed, shortly return on the clouds to judge the world and inaugurate the new age. The central story is embellished and illustrated by peripheral legends which tell of miracles and wonders, voices from heaven, victories over demons, and the like. These legends belong to 'myth', the undifferentiated discourse of a prescientific age, when events both in the world of men and in the world of nature were assigned to the direct agency of occult force whether divine or demonic.[10]

Bultmann in his book *Primitive Christianity in its Contemporary Setting* expounded his theological project by showing that many of the theological ideas which became central to the Christian faith were not unique to the community of faith, but were collected and interwoven by Christians, from the mystery religions and influential trends of the philosophical thought of the Graeco-Roman world in the first four centuries of the Christian era.[11] However, many Christians today do not accept this extreme view that the Jesus of history is impossible for the modern Christian to encounter, nor do they accept wholly the suggestion that the scriptural accounts of the historical existence, almost two thousand years ago, were entirely mythologized by the early Christian community. The fact is, as Colin Brown has observed, that 'The only Christ we know of is the Christ who is witnessed by Scripture and who endorsed the integrity of Scripture.'

Bultmann's project of making the Christian faith more credible to modern scientific man does not succeed in reducing the Christ of Faith to the Jesus of History through demythologization because such a project, if it succeeded, would reduce religious faith to the level of a scientific hypothesis, and we have already seen, in our earlier discussion of deductive and inductive reasoning, that the probability reached through scientific calculations cannot correctly be taken to be conceptually identical with the absoluteness of religious faith.

The two mutually critical and extreme theological positions have been challenged by another of Barth's contemporary theologians — Dietrich Bonhoeffer — whom it would be worthwhile to cite before proceeding further with our consideration of theology as contextual response. His few theological writings have become greatly influential in another significant trend in twentieth-century Western theology, especially the published collection of his *Letters and Papers*. The following is a brief critical comment by Bonhoeffer on the theological projects of Barth and Bultmann:

> Bultmann would seem to have felt Barth's limitations in some way, but he misconstrues them in the light of liberal theology, and hence goes off into the typical liberal reduction process (the "mythological" elements of Christianity are dropped, and Christianity is reduced to its 'essence'). I am of the view that the full content, including the mythological concepts, must be maintained. The New Testament is not a mythological garbing of the universal truth: this mythology (resurrection and so on) is the thing itself — but the concepts must be interpreted in such a way as not to make religion a pre-condition of faith (cf. circumcision in St. Paul). Not until that is achieved will, in my opinion, liberal theology be overcome (and even Barth is still dominated by it, though negatively), and, at the same time, the question it raises be genuinely taken up and answered — which is not the case in the positivism of revelation maintained by the Confessing Church.[12]

Bonhoeffer was making a contextual theological response, in which he addressed himself to the question as to what it meant, in practical terms, to be a Christian in Germany during the time of Hitler. We need not delve into an elaboration of his ideas, though some of them would be very interesting to discuss — such as his suggestions that 'man has come of age', and that what was needed in his existential situation was a 'religionless Christianity'. He did not live long enough to expound these and other themes. However, our reference to the quotation from his *Letters and Papers* serves to show the fundamental problem inherent in either of the two views of the Bible as the Word of God.

The Barthian and Bultmannian positions are, I think, at the opposite ends of the broad spectrum of Christian theological views in contemporary Western theology. In our citation, Bonhoeffer has shown that neither position, taken in its extremity, provides a conclusive and satisfactory solution to the question of the practical meaning of Christian Revelation. Nevertheless, an understanding of the contextual setting of Barth's and Bultmann's theological projects (characterized, for instance, by liberalism, biblical criticism and positivism) would help us to appreciate their contributions to contemporary Western Christian theology.

But neither of them, nor any other, should form the fundamental framework for contemporary African Christian theological reflection, partly because the contextual setting of contemporary Africa is different from that of Barth and Bultmann, and partly because the African Christian should make his own direct response to the Gospel, without the necessity of apprehending the Christian message merely from the reflections or refractions of other people's responses, even though some such responses may be stimulating and encouraging.

Our allusion to three Western theologians of the same generation (arbitrarily selected for the purpose of this discussion) has served to show that theological discourse is a process in which the theologians of one period respond to, and are influenced by, the philosophical and theological ideas of preceding generations, and that their own contributions in turn continue to influence, positively or negatively, future generations of theologians. Such is what African theological discourse also is, and should be — it is not an event which is to be accomplished once and for all, but a continuing endeavour which began long ago, and will go on long into the distant future, with varying degrees of intensity. The allusion has shown also that within a particular existential situation, there may be not one uniform trend of theological interpretation, but that there could be even diametrically opposed theological positions constituting the theological discourse of the time and place. Likewise, it would be absurd to expect uniformity and homogeneity in the development of African Christian theology, whether continentally or within the particularities of the local Churches in different parts of Africa.

The most positive attitude in this great endeavour is, I think, for each

Christian theologian to treat with respect and appreciation the interpretations of others, with the objective of a constructive contribution rather than destructive discouragement. The Christian message is much more profound than any one person's understanding of it, and much more extensive in its implications than all the articulated interpretations put together. If this were not the case, the Gospel would not have the universal appeal that it has . This does not necessarily imply that any theological viewpoint is correct, nor should it lead to the conclusion that all theological interpretations which are articulated in a particular time and a particular place carry the same degree of intensity and relevance. But it does demand that restraint and fairness should be exercised when a person makes assessments and judgements about the theological positions of others. 'Judge not, that you be not judged. For with the judgement you pronounce you will be judged, and the measure you give will be the measure you get. Why do you see the speck that is in your brother's eye, but do not notice the log that is in your own eye? You hypocrite, first take the log out of your eye, and then you will see clearly to take the speck out of your brother's eye' (Matt. 7:1–5).

If this teaching were heeded and taken seriously, much of the denomination-al exclusiveness and complacency which keeps many Christian Churches divided today would be considerably reduced. In bridging the gaps and fostering mutual understanding between denominations, the modern ecume-nical movement has a great role to fulfil. It also has a great task to encourage the growth of understanding between Christians and people of other religious traditions.

NOTES

1. James H. Cone, *The Spirituals and the Blues*, New York: Seabury Press, 1972; Gayraud S. Wilmore, *Black Religion and Black Radicalism*, New York: Doubleday, 1973.

2. Placide Tempels, *Bantu Philosophy*, Paris: Presence Africaine, Eng. Ed., 1959, p. 36.

3. J.S. Mbiti, *The Crisis of Mission in Africa*, Mukono, Uganda: Uganda Church Press, 1971.

4. Colin Brown, *Philosophy and the Christian Faith*, Dovers Grove Illinois: Inter-Varsity Press, 1968, pp. 251–2.

5. Bertrand Russel, *The Problems of Philosophy*, London: Oxford University Press, 1959, pp. 33–38.

6. Bertrand Russel, *History of Western Philosophy*, London: Allen and Unwin, 1946, 2nd ed. 1961, pp. 520–21; J.G. Donders, *Don't Fence Us In: The Liberating Power of Philosophy*, 11th Inaugural Lecture, University of Nairobi, 1975.

7. For a discussion of the Theory of Evolution from a theological and philosophical perspective see J.N.K. Mugambi, *God, Humanity and Nature in Relation to Justice and Peace*, Geneva: World Council of Churches, 1987. There still are some Christians who would like to treat the doctrine of creation as a scientific hypothesis, but such treatment makes the Genesis narrative a very poor scientific account which would not pass the tests of empirical verification. See, for example, C.H. McGowen, *In Six Days*, Van Nuys, California: Bible Voice, 1976.

8. *Awake*, March 8, 1978, New York: Watchtower Bible and Tract Society, p. 32.

9. Colin Brown, *op.cit.*, p. 254.

10. John Macquarrie, *Twentieth Century Religious Thought*, London SCM Press, 1962, p. 362.

11. Rudolf Bultmann, *Primitive Christianity in its Contemporary Setting*, London/Glasgow, Collins/Fontana, 1960.

12. Dietrich Bonhoeffer, *Letters and Papers from Prison*, London Glasgow, Collins/Fontana, 1959, p. 110.

Chapter Three

CHRISTIAN RESPONSE
IN DEHUMANIZING SITUATIONS

Christianity as a Proclamation of Hope

Ideally, Christianity as a religion based on the teaching of Jesus of Nazareth proclaims a message of hope following its founder, who announced:

> The Spirit of the Lord is upon me, because he has anointed me to preach good news to the poor. He has sent me to proclaim release to the captives and recovering of sight to the blind, to set at liberty those who are oppressed, to proclaim the acceptable year of the Lord (Luke 4:18-19, Isaiah 61:1-2).[1]

The concern of proclaiming hope is expressed here as an ideal because, in practice, it is not always that the Church has been fulfilling that challenging commitment laid down by Jesus for himself and his followers. For example, when Christianity became the fashionable official religion in Europe after the conversion of Emperor Constantine and in the declining Roman empire, the Catholic Church became an oppressive structure which ruthlessly suppressed those people who did not conform to its teaching and practice. This post-Constantinian intolerance of the Church lingered on for many centuries, and partly contributed to the rise of the Reformation.[2] Reformed Christianity, however, did not entirely abandon this attitude of intolerance.[3]

Today, intolerance and a lack of mutual appreciation among the numerous Christian denominations are significant factors which hinder the universal Church from making a greater positive impact in the contemporary world.[4] The ecumenical movement, with all the problems it faces, is involved in a worthwhile endeavour towards reconciliation which comes after the freedom of individuals and groups in society has been fully respected.[5]

Jesus practically proclaimed reconciliation based on mutual recognition and appreciation of the dignity and full humanity of all men and women. Peace on earth (Luke 2:14) can be realized fuly only in global situations where the goals expressed in the prophetic passage quoted above are experienced. The theme of the WCC Fifth Assembly (Nairobi, November–December 1975) — 'Jesus Christ Frees and Unites' — was a precise echo of that prophetic and encouraging passage which Jesus read in the book of Isaiah, and fulfilled with all his life. The extent to which Christians implement this message of hope practically will indicate the degree of their faithfulness to the Master's call to discipleship. As Dietrich Bonhoeffer courageously showed with his life, work and writings, the cost of Christian discipleship is great, but it is a cost worth paying for the sake of human freedom, justice and reconciliation, which are basic ingredients of lasting peace on earth.

When Jesus had read this remarkable passage, he added in his own words: 'Today this scripture has been fulfilled in your hearing.' (Luke 4:21). A prophecy is fulfilled when the events expressed in it are realized. Thus by reading this passage and announcing its fulfilment Jesus pledged to make it a living reality. From prison, John the Baptist later sent his disciples to enquire of Jesus if He was the Messiah who had been anticipated in Old Testament prophecy. Jesus replied: 'Go and tell John what you have seen and heard: the blind receive their sight, the lame walk, lepers are cleansed, and the deaf hear, the dead are raised up, the poor have good news preached to them. And blessed is he who takes no offence at me'. (Luke 7:18–23). Actions speak louder than words, and Jesus made his actions speak louder than words, to the extent that his followers recognized him 'as one who had authority, not as the scribes'. (Mark 1:22). The Church, as the community of the followers of Jesus, is challenged to respond to all dehumanizing situations in such a way that its actions speak louder than its verbal proclamations. Otherwise its message of hope, which is echoed from Jesus, will lose credibility among those who need hope and encouragement in situations which have brought them to the verge of despair.

Dehumanizing Situations

A dehumanizing situation is one in which human beings are hindered from realizing their full humanity. Dehumanizing situations exist in human society in many forms and are experienced in almost all historical contexts. In that prophetic passage which Jesus quoted from Isaiah, Jesus outlined the following situations as dehumanizing ones: poverty, captivity, oppression, prejudice, physical illness, and estrangement from God. Jesus dealt with all these situations in his earthly ministry, illustrating how his followers were to respond to such situations in society. The reply of Jesus to the disciples of John the Baptist when they came to enquire if he was the Messiah referred to his work in alleviating physical illness among the individuals in his community.

However, in his total ministry Jesus was deeply concerned with elimination of all dehumanization. Considered as a whole, his metaphors, parables and analogies about the 'Kingdom of God' anticipate the situation in which all dehumanization would end, so that human beings would enjoy their full humanity as 'Children of God' without any hindrances.

Jesus inaugurated the 'Kingdom of God' free from all dehumanization and he charged his followers with the challenging responsibility of continuing the work of renewal which he had begun and to which he was totally committed. It is a great theological mistake for the Church to concentrate on any one particular form of dehumanization while ignoring other forms, because Jesus was concerned with humanization of the *whole person* in the context of the *whole society*. Therefore, when a prophetic voice or movement draws the Church's attention to aspects of dehumanization which may have been neglected, the Church has a theological obligation to heed such correction in order to overcome any shortcomings in its Christian ministry. It is worthwhile to cite a few other references in the teaching of Jesus which illustrate the variety of dehumanizing situations to which Christians are challenged to respond positively and practically.

While he was commenting about the 'Kingdom of God' in one of his sermons, Jesus said:

'When the Son of Man comes in his glory and all the angels with him then he will sit on his glorious throne. Before him will be gathered all the nations, and he will separate them one from another as a shepherd separates the sheep from the goats, and he will place the sheep at his right hand, but the goats at the left. Then the king will say to those at his right hand, "Come, O blessed of my Father, inherit the kingdom prepared for you from the foundation of the world; for I was hungry and you gave me food, I was thirsty and you gave me drink, I was a stranger and you welcomed me, I was naked and you clothed me, I was sick and you visited me, I was in prison and you came to me." Then the righteous will answer him, "Lord, when did we see thee hungry and feed thee, or thirsty and give thee drink? And when did we see thee a stranger and welcome thee, or naked and clothed thee? And when did we see thee sick or in prison and visited thee?" And the king will answer them, "Truly, I say to you, as you did it to one of the least of these my brethen, you did it to me.'" (Matt. 25:31–40)

This passage outlines another set of dehumanizing situations and reinforces dehumanization which Jesus had attacked when he quoted the hopeful prophecy of Isaiah. In his ministry, Jesus fulfilled the demands of the 'Kingdom of God' which are expected in this passage. Literally, he fed the hungry (Mark 8:1–10), gave those who were thirsty drink (John 2:1–12), welcomed strangers (John 4:1–42), and so on. That he visited strangers and prisoners is not very obvious, but his relationship with Zacchaeus (Luke 19:1–10) and Nicodemus (John 3:1–12) can be seen as an illustration of this concern. These two men were prisoners in their status. Jesus was criticized for interacting with Zacchaeus, and Nicodemus had to see Jesus at night because as a ruler (leader) he feared being seen with Jesus who was mingling with the lower members of the society. The interaction of Jesus with those who were regarded as 'untouchables' is a constant reminder to the Church that Christians ought to identify themselves, as followers of Jesus, with those people who have become dehumanized as victims of various forms of prejuce. It is instructive to consider this theme of *prejudice* more closely.

Prejudice

A situation in which prejudice thrives is one where in a society one social group regards itself as being superior to others, and on the basis of this assumed superiority discriminates against those people whom it considers inferior. Prejudice may be entrenched on the basis of economic, ethnic or political groupings. Sometimes it is reinforced through a combination of all these three factors, as has been the case in South Africa. The situation in which prejudice of any kind is entrenched in society is a very dehumanizing one. When a person is forced to feel that he is less human than others because of his ethnic identity, political status or economic status, he greatly suffers from such dehumanization.

Jesus condemned all forms of prejudice, and he attacked it by freely mingling with those people who were regarded as being inferior members of his community. In his teaching, he showed that the victims of prejudice were as human as, and often more so than, those who assumed themselves to be the superiors. A few scriptural examples will illustrate this point. In the time of Jesus, official Judaism tended to set up barriers of social status between Jews and Samaritans (John 4:1–42), between Jews and Gentiles (Matt. 5:47, 6:32), and also political barriers between Jews and the Roman authorities with their administrative agents (Matt. 22:15–22, Mark 2:15–17).

The parable of the Good Samaritan is theologically significant not only because of the compassion which was extended to a suffering person, but also because it was a Samaritan — a member of a despised ethnic group — who acted righteously in a context where those who claimed to be most righteous failed to demonstrate their piety practically. This parable illustrates the folly and vanity of religious hypocrisy that is disguised in professed piety (Luke 10:29–37). When he gave this parable, Jesus was answering a question he had been asked about good neighbourliness. A good neighbour, according to this parable, is one who responds positively to help those in need, rather than one who lives in one's neighbourhood or belongs to one's religion, ethnic group or economic status. The Samaritan, in spite of his despised ethnic identity, was the one who proved to be the good neighbour to the person who fell victim among robbers.

Prejudice is sustained by false pride, false confidence and complacency. It thrives in fear, because those who regard themselves as superiors are always afraid lest the privileges they enjoy forcefully be lost when those whom they oppress regain their freedom to realize the humanization which prejudice denies them. This fear leads to more oppression, violence and also dehumanization, as the self-proclaimed superiors endeavour to maintain their privileges while their victims continue to struggle in order to regain their *freedom* to live as human beings. The tensions which build up in the context of this struggle generate what Helder Camara has called the 'spiral of violence'. The more the oppressors cling to and enforce their privileges, the more the victims of oppression in that context yearn and struggle for freedom.

The Vicious Circles of Violence

The spiral of violence generated by prejudice cannot be stopped merely by appealing to the oppressed to succumb to their oppressors because the struggles of the victims of oppression are struggles for survival, for justice and for freedom. The violence of oppressors is violence to safeguard luxury, whereas the violence of the victims of oppression is a reaction against oppression, a necessary struggle for survival under those circumstances. The vicious circle of violence which results from prejudice can be broken either by the oppressors abandoning their oppressive measures and respecting the freedom and humanity of their victims in the name of justice, or by the continuation of the struggle for survival and freedom by the victims of oppression until they regain their humanity.[7]

The issue of violence and non-violence is, therefore, a subsidiary one. Survival, freedom, justice and humanization are logically and theologically prior to the question of violence and non-violence. Jesus did not identify himself with the Zealots, but this does not mean that he favoured the continued subjugation of his people under the Roman empire. He refused to participate in the military overthrow of the Roman rule, but this does not mean that he was in favour of the status quo. Neither he nor his disciples organized peaceful protest demonstrations in the streets of the towns of Judea, but this does not mean that he was indifferent to the yearning of his people for freedom. Jesus was a pacifist in the sense that he favoured and worked for peace based on genuine reconciliation.

Human dignity is a precondition for freedom, and freedom is a precondition for reconciliation. Without the full realization of one's dignity, one cannot experience full freedom, and without the realization of full freedom, there can be no basis for a deep initiative towards reconciliation. Hence Jesus worked for the restoration of eroded human dignity among the victims of oppression in his society, because this, in his teaching, was as basic a requirement as the beginning of the process of reconciliation. Without reconciliation there can be no genuine peace and, therefore, in the teaching of Jesus, the restoration of eroded human dignity is the first step towards peace on earth, and towards the 'Kingdom of God'.[8]

Since the restoration of human dignity and freedom are preconditions for effective and genuine reconciliation, there can be no genuine reconciliation between a slave and his master, as long as the master-slave relationship is maintained. It is human to crave for survival, freedom and justice and as long as any of these rights is denied or threatened, situations of dehumanization will continue to hinder the realization of genuine peace.

If it is the will of God that all people should be free and reconciled to one another, as Jesus taught, then the Church has an obligation to work diligently, following Jesus, for the realization of freedom. Those people who suffer under the yokes of all forms of dehumanization are hindered from realizing freedom, and Christians are charged with the responsibility of responding practically by contributing towards the establishment of the "Kingdom of God" as a promise which will be experienced in the future in "Heaven", it will lose its credibility as a proclamation of hope.

Therefore, it is consistent with the ideal teaching of Christianity that the followers of Jesus ought to identify themselves with the victims of all forms of dehumanization rather than with those who invent or maintain dehumanizing situations.

The Church has an obligation to endeavour to make its practice as identical as possible with this ideal which Jesus practically fulfilled. The details of what practical contribution Christians in particular contexts can make towards the elimination of dehumanization — towards the 'Kingdom of God' — must be left to the Christians themselves, to exercise their freedom under the guidance of the Holy Spirit and the Christian scriptures. (The epistle to the Galatians is relevant here, because of its elaboration of Christian liberty.) A *passive* proclamation of the "GOOD NEWS" of hope is a distortion of Christian discipleship, because in Jesus of Nazareth whom Christians affirm to be Christ, Son of God, verbal proclamation was inseparable from practical implementation. Jesus fulfilled what he verbally taught. Likewise, the Church and Christian organizations ought to endeavour to fulfil in practice what they preach in theory, following the example of Jesus. In that way, the Church will contribute effectively towards the elimination of dehumanizing situations, towards the realization of peace on earth.

Is the realization of peace on earth identical with the final establishment of the 'Kingdom of God?' This is an important theological question which we cannot discuss in detail here without digressing from the main theme of this chapter. But the question must be asked because the Christian response in dehumanizing situations is directly related to the Christian anticipation of the 'Kingdom of God'. No one can expect to enter the 'Kingdom of God' if he does not work conscientiously for peace on earth (Matt. 5:19).

Varieties of Practical Contribution Towards the Alleviation of Dehumanization

Throughout its history, the Christian Church has recognized that God has bestowed a variety of gifts on human individuals. During the first century AD, St. Paul wrote to the Corinthian Christians:

Now there are varieties of gifts, but the same spirit; and there are varieties of service, but it is the same God; and there are varieties of working, but it is the same God who inspires them all in everyone. To each is given the manifestation of the Spirit for the common good. To one is given through the Spirit the utterance of wisdom, and to another the utterance of knowledge according to the same Spirit, to another faith by the same Spirit, to another gifts of hearing by the one prophecy, to another various kinds of gifts to distinguish between spirits, to another various kinds of tongues, to another the interpretation of tongues. All these are inspired by one and the same Spirit, who apportions to each one individual as he wills (1 Cor. 12:1–11).

In the same chapter, Paul continues to emphasize that the body consists of many organs, each with its own function but all organs functioning to enhance the life of the whole body (1 Cor. 12:12–27). Expressing his emphasis more concretely in the context of the Corinthian Church, Paul added:

And God has appointed in the Church first apostles, second prophets, third teachers, then workers of miracles, then healers, administrators, speakers in various kinds of tongues. Are all apostles? Are all teachers? Do all work miracles? Do all possess gifts of healing? Do all speak with tongues? Do all interpret? But earnestly desire the higher gifts (1 Cor. 12:28–31).

This part of Paul's first epistle to the Corinthians may help us to discern some positive insights concerning the variety of contributions that Christians can make towards the alleviation of dehumanization in the world. Jesus combined in his ministry many of the roles that Paul listed — prophecy, preaching, teaching, healing, performing miracles and so on. Few ordinary human individuals are bestowed with such a wide range of gifts. Our human limitations condition us to contribute the most that we can manage within those limitations. But Paul cautions us to avoid dictating to other people what they should do, especially when they are working *with* us towards common goals. If the common goal is the elimination of dehumanizing situations — the realization of the 'Kingdom of God' in all its dimensions — then we need to appreciate the contributions of all those who earnestly work toward this goal.

It needs no emphasizing that, within a particular socio-political context, a combination of efforts is required from all those people committed to improve conditions towards more humanization. Theologically, it is erroneous to limit commendable Christian activity to only one mode of operation. Jesus did not limit his ministry to just one mode of activity — rather, he conducted and integrated the ministry which he also entrusted to his followers. The Christian Church claims to follow this apostolic responsibility and should, in agreement with Paul's insights regarding the Christian ministry, serve God in the world according to this integrated approach.

The comments made so far concerning the ideal Christian response to dehumanizing situations have concentrated upon the ministry of the Church *within* particular socio-political contexts. But what can Christians living *outside such contexts* contribute? To this question we shall now turn.

The Church is sometimes defined as 'the New Israel' and as 'the New People of God' (Rom. 4:12-25). Theologically these designations are disturbing, even though Paul used them in a particular context when he was challenging the complacency of the Jews in their relationship with non-Jews. In what sense are Christians the 'people of God?' Do these designations imply that non-Christians are not God's people? If this were the implication, a serious contradiction would be logically evident in Christian doctrine. Christianity teaches that God is the creator of the entire human race. How can a section of humanity be regarded in another doctrine of the same religion as people who do not 'belong to God?' Is it necessary for Christians who favour these designations to clarify what they understand by the expression 'people of God?' Owing to the use of these designations, another problem has been in defining 'God's work'. There has been a tendency to regard 'God's work as that which is done within the Church. The ministry of Jesus does not justify such a limited definition of 'God's work'.

Material Contributions — Goods and Money

During the first century AD, various Churches in the Mediterranean region functioned as social entities, each with its own identity. Each had its particular problems. Although all of them were generally under one imperial authority with its capital in Rome, the particular problems faced by Christians differed from Church to Church. This was why St. Paul felt it necessary to write Epistles addressed to particular Christian communities and individuals helping them overcome their particular challenges. At the same time, however, these Christian communities felt committed to maintain a unity based on their common faith in Jesus and on their mutual concern for the welfare of one another. This unity was not merely abstract and metaphysical — it was real and practical.

The various congregations prayed for one another, and shared their concern to maintain a doctrinal consensus. One of the most significant illustrations of this real mutual concern was evidenced in the Council of Jerusalem (Acts Ch. 15, Gal, Chs. 2-3) in which the Church leaders and missionaries from various Christian communities discerned a doctrinal concensus on the question as to how Christians could maintain common witness of the faith in a world full of cultural diversity. This sense of mutual concern was also maintained at the practical and material level, especially when one community was faced with particular material needs. Other communities not only prayed and encouraged the one in difficulty, but they also sent material help to that congregation.

This practical concern in the early Church is illustrated by the material contributions which Paul was collecting for the purpose of helping the Church in Jerusalem. A paragraph in the introduction to Paul's epistle to the Romans in the *Oxford Annotated Bible* (RSV) remarks:

> For several years — of intense missionary activity and of more than ordinary stress — Paul had been engaged in collecting contributions from the Gentile Churches of Greece and Asia Minor for the needy Jerusalem Church. It was his hope that these gifts would allay certain suspicions of him and his work which some members of that Church felt and which had been a source of anxiety to him. The collection was now complete, and Paul, apparently in Corinth . . . was awaiting an opportunity to go to Jerusalem with it.[9]

Paul himself explained the importance of contributing such material help in 2 Cor. 8:1–5:15. It is important to emphasize that this relief was not merely for Christian 'saints' in Jerusalem. It was for further re-distribution to the needy in Palestine (2 Cor. 8:1–9:15). Contributions in kind helped in strengthening the mutual concern which had been expressed verbally, thus unifying theory with practice, as Jesus had been doing in his ministry.

Christianity has spread far beyond the Mediterranean region to all the six continents of the world. If the same sense of unity, concern and mutual responsibility is to be maintained as was done in the early Church, verbal proclamations must be supported with material contribution. Support must extend beyond sympathy, encouragement, comfort and prayer.

Material contributions may be only tokens of appreciation of the suffering of others, but they are significant indications of genuine love and concern. Material help should be sent wherever there is suffering, irrespective of whether the victims of dehumanization are Christian or not. This is a motto which is in accordance with the concern of Jesus to inaugurate an era in which dehumanization would be conquered. Material help should not be sent 'with strings attached', be they strings of exerting influence or winning more members for the donating denomination!

In today's world, money has become one of the most important mediums of economic exchange. With money, goods can be bought and transferred from one country to another within a short time. In a world with a wide cultural diversity and ranging political interests, it may sometimes be more effective to contribute money rather than send relief in form of goods. Money will enable those in need to buy goods of their choice, whereas relief in form of goods conditions the beneficiaries to consume the goods donated even though the donations may be culturally inappropriate in the recipient's context.

It is true that money may be misappropriated by the recipients. But the same can happen to relief in form of goods — the material relief may not, for example, reach the intended recipients. In some Christian circles, it has been argued that money given as contribution toward efforts for the elimination of dehumanizing situations may be used for buying arms which are used in escalating violence. The implication in this argument is that money should not be given to those organizations which are involved in violent activities. The argument has been inconsistent, because while it was against the victims of institutional violence, it gave moral support to violent regimes. The controversial debate that has surrounded the WCC Programme to Combat Racism is a case in point. It has already been remarked that when the debate is shifted to its proper perspective, shifted from a discussion of violence and non-violence to the concern for the elimination of dehumanization in the world, the significance of organizations like the Programme to Combat Racism becomes more evident.[10]

While it is true that today's world is full of problems which cannot be considered identical with those experienced in the first century AD in the Mediterranean region, it is also true that Jesus, and the apostolic Church after him, offered material contribution to alleviate dehumanizing situations. This is an insight which Christians cannot afford to ignore without losing the essence of Christian discipleship.

It is better to give material contributions in form of goods and money, bearing the risk that some of the contributions might be misappropriated, than to stay idle and leave the victims of dehumanization to continue suffering. Discretion must be left to the donors, who must bear the responsibility of applying the principle of Christian liberty. At the same time, however, there must be mutual trust between the donor and the recipient of aid, otherwise the donor organizes policing mechanisms to look after his aid, thereby restricting further the freedom and the humanization of the recipient.

NOTES

1. For discussion of the "acceptable year of the Lord" — Jubilee, see Howard Yoder, *The Politics of Jesus,* Grand Rapids, Michigan: Eerdmans, 1975; Hans Jochen Boecker, *Law and the Administration of Justice in the Old Testament and Ancient East,* London: SPCK, 1980, pp. 88–108, *The Interpreter's Bible,* Vol. II, Nashville: Abingdon, 1953, 1981, pp. 121–23.

2. Religious intolerance during the Dark Ages in Europe seems to have been motivated primarily by the desire to maintain unity of belief and practice at a time when the Roman empire was disintegrating from within and under attack from all directions. See H. A.L. Fisher, *A History of Europe, Vol. 1, From the Earliest Time to 1713,* London/Glasgow: Collins/Fontana, 1935; E.R. Hardy, "The Mission of the Church in the First Four Centuries" in *History's Lessons for Tomorrow's Mission,* Geneva: World Student Christian Federation, C. 1960, pp. 29–38; Hans-Jochen Margull, "The Awakening of Protestant Mission", in *History's Lessons for Tomorrow's Mission, op.cit.,* pp. 137–48.

3. Hans-Jochen Margull, *art.cit.,* pp. 147–48.

4. The achievement of unity has been one of the perennial challenges of the Universal Church. At the Council of Jerusalem (Acts ch. 15 and Gal. ch. 2–3) St. Paul managed to guide the delegates towards a consensus over the admission of Gentiles into the Christian Church. Today, the Modern Ecumenical movement strives towards a consensus, but is continually attacked by those who would prefer to maintain a divided church. On this problem see W.A. Vissert'Hooft, *Has the Ecumenical Movement a Future?* Belfst: Christian Journals Ltd., 1974; Leon Howell, *Acting in Faith:* The WCC since 1975, Geneva: WCC, 1982; *Sharing in one Hope: Bangalore 1878* — Reports and Documents from the meeting of the Faith and Order Commission, Geneva: WCC, Faith and Order Paper No. 92, 1978; on the opposing viewpoint see Norvald Yri, *Quest for Authority:* An Investigation into the Quest for Authority within the Ecumenical Movement from 1910 to 1974 and the Evangelical Response.

5. Freedom logically and practically precedes genuine reconciliation. Only genuine free parties can be genuinely reconciled to one another. There can be no genuine reconciliation between a master and his slave as long as the condition of slavery is maintained between them. The freedom of choice and action must be respected before the process of reconciliation can commence. This insight underlies the teaching of Paul in Gal. 3:28. It was the theological and philosophical foundation of the theme of the WCC 5th Assembly in Nairobi, Kenya, Nov–Dec. 1985 — "Jesus Christ Frees and Unites".

6. Dietrich Bonhoeffer, *The Cost of Discipleship*, Revised Edition, New York Macmillan, 1963; *Letters and Papers From Prison*, op.cit., *Ethics*, London/Glasgow: Collins/-Fontana, 1964.

7. This point is lucidly articulated in *Racism in Theology and Theology Against Racism*, Geneva: World Council of Churches, 1975; see also A.J. van der Bent, *Incarnation and New Creation: The Ecumenical Movement at Crossroads*, Madras, India: Christian Literature society, 1986, pp. 59-68; Leon Howell, *Acting in Faith op.cit., pp. 74-83*.

8. Dietrich Bonhoeffer emphasizes that freedom and responsibility are logically and practically inseparable. From the end of responsibility, the responsible person must exercise his freedom responsibly, while respecting and appreciating the freedom of others. From the end of freedom, the free person must limit the exercise of his responsibility in order to facilitate the exercise and experience of freedom by others. This is a very helpful insight in the context of the present chapter. See Dietrich Bonhoeffer, *Ethics*, London/Glasgow: Collins/Fontana, 1964, pp. 248-62. *Letters and Papers, op.cit., pp. 148-53, 161-63, The Cost of Discipleship, op.cit.*

9. *Oxford Annotated Bible*, p. 1359.

10. Elisabeth Adler, *A Small Beginning*, op.cit.

Chapter Four

RESPONSE OF THE CHURCH
TO CRISES IN AFRICA

Introduction

The 'response' to a situation may be active or passive; it can be a confrontation, a retreat or an accommodation. 'Church' is a word that carries many meanings, and it would be necessary to explain how one intends to use it before embarking on any discussion about the 'Church'. The word 'crisis' also conveys a variety of meanings, depending on those who use it and the situations that are labelled with this word. The main part of this chapter will concentrate on explaining the various ways in which these terms can be understood in the African context. Even the term 'Africa' needs to be explained After these explanations some normative suggestions will be offered, on the basis of what we consider to be preferential options appropriate for our situation in contemporary Africa.

The Church and Its Many Facets

In the New Testament, the Christian Community is described both in singular and plural terms. Jesus expected his disciples to be the agents or messengers who would facilitate the establishment and spread of the Church (singular).[1] Paul wrote his epistles to Christian communities (Churches) in various parts of the Mediterranean region. Thus we note that singularity and plurality are real characteristics of the Christian Community.

The individual believer does not singly form the Church, and yet without individual believers there can be no Church. This is another paradoxical charateristic of the Christian Community.

As a social organism, the Church is susceptible to all the challenges faced by social institutions, and yet its claim to divine authority is often considered to absolve the Church from fallibility. The Church exists *in this world,* to witness to the Kingdom of God which *is not of this world.*[2] Pilate could not understand 'the truth' of which Jesus came to bear witness.[3] Yet the culmination of Jesus' ministry was crucifixion, a form of execution which was devised to purge Roman society of wrongdoers. At the social level, the Church exists paradoxically as both a corrective and an offensive institution.

These few observations about the Church lead us to affirm that it is an organism that is too complex to be described simplistically. It may be likened to a diamond crystal which refracts many different colours of light from every direction. Each facet of the crystal shows a different combination of colours, and yet all the variety is in the same crystal. As a living social organism, the Church displays even greater variety, because it changes in membership, location and in history. The Epistles illustrate this point clearly. Paul found it necessary to write different letters to respective Christian communities. To some of them he wrote more than one letter, dealing with problems that had arisen in the meantime. Yet Paul emphasized that all these communities were members of the same one Church, founded on Jesus Christ.

Within the Church, there are the official leaders, recognized as the representatives and spokesmen of the social organism. In the secular context, there is a tendency to regard these as the official Church. However, the leadership can represent the ordinary members only to a limited extent. Each member remains responsible for his own beliefs and his own actions, irrespective of what the official leaders of his Church may publicly declare. Official declarations are not substitutes for individual decisions and action. At the same time, collective decisions and actions within the context of the Church strengthen the impact of their individual responsibility.

Thus there is a sense in which the official leadership is the Church, as far as the social function of the Christian community is concerned. Yet the ordinary members are also the Church because without them the official leaders would have nobody to represent. The existential paradox is clear.

In another sense, the Church is manifested by the 'salt' and 'light' within the Christian community. A few committed believers keep the Church 'ticking', both within the ordinary membership and within the leadership. Those who are the 'salt' and 'light' may not realize that indeed they are; but the challenge of Jesus Christ is that all his disciples must strive to be the light and salt in the world. So not everyone in the Church is its 'salt' and 'light', and yet without these few who serve this role, the Church would become insignificant and irrelevant in society.

What, then, is the Church? Or *who* is the Church? In one sense, all those who call themselves Christians are the Church. But in another sense, none of them are (Rom. 12:3–8; 1 Cor. 12:4–31). It is advisable to discern the role of each facet of the Church, and the implication of each existential paradox as we have observed earlier. Only then can we begin to appreciate what it means to be the Church in the World in general and in Africa in particular.

The Problem of Crisis – Identification

According to the *Advanced Learner's Dictionary of Current English*, 'crisis' is a noun referring to a turning point in illness, life, history, etc; a time of difficulty, danger or anxiety about the future.

A person who faints or collapses owing to a stroke will be at a critical point in his life, but he may not realize this until he regains consciousness. One of the paradoxes of human existence is that we do not realize that we are in crisis until the critical point is crossed. Sometimes we do not even notice when we have gone through crisis. Other people may advise us that we have been in critical situations, but we may disagree with such advice, depending on our own position.

As human beings, we have a tendency to notice the crises others are going through and to ignore our own. The ideal would be for us to anticipate crises so as to prevent them, yet this we seem incapable of doing. Whenever we organize ourselves to prevent a crisis, we tend to create a new crisis in turn. Jesus offered the following advice: 'Judge not, that you may not be judged, as the measure you give will be the measure you get. Why do you see the *speck* that is in your brother's eye, but do not notice the *log* that is in your own eye? Or how can you say to your brother, "Let me take the *speck* out of your eye," when there is a *log* in your own eye? You hypocrite, first take the log out of your eye, and then you will see clearly to take the *speck* out of your brother's eye!' (Matt. 7:1–5, RSV).[4]

The problem of crisis-identifications is condensed in this teaching of Jesus. As a problem of our human nature, it is manifested by our tendency to rush to declare that other people are in crisis, before we even admit that we ourselves are in deeper crises. We tend to console ourselves by bailing other people from their minor crisis, before we have even admitted the depth and gravity of our own crisis.

Jesus advises that the way out of this problem is for us to be always self-critical and self-analytical. We ought to acknowledge our own failures and weaknesses before we go out to condemn and blame others. This advice makes existential and pragmatic sense. Yet most of us find it difficult to live by it, perhaps because we fear facing the reality about ourselves.

In the context of contemporary Africa, outsiders have told Africans what crises Africa is in. But sometimes Africans have not understood their situation as outsiders have described it. Who will decide when there is a conflict of interpretation? In the contemporary world, it appears that the old adage applies: Whoever pays the piper calls the tune. Yet the weight of one's purse does not match one's musical taste. The gold and silver in the purse may confuse the sensitive ear, or drown a rhythmic melody. Africans ought to be self-critical of their own situation, and outsiders should listen more and talk less than they have done in the past. Africa's colonial history does not augur well for this approach, and yet we have to learn from the past in order to build a more promising future. Masters must appreciate what it means to be a slave.

There is a difference in the priorities listed by Africans and those listed by their former colonial masters, with regard to the crises facing Africa. The former emphasize over-population, over-grazing, illiteracy, malnutrition and such negative factors. The Africans themselves view these as symptoms rather than as the causes of their problems. From the African perspective, liberation in its total sense is the greatest aspiration. As long as Africans are not free to determine their own destiny, they will remain in deep crises — crises of identity, crises of self-determination, crises of economic self-reliance, and so on.

The treatment of symptoms cannot cure a disease. If the current crises in Africa are to be overcome, their root causes must be identified. The Africans themselves will have to do this for themselves, and find out what has gone wrong. Only the wearer knows where the shoe pinches, as the old adage says.

Responses of Christian Churches to Crises in Africa

In view of the observations we have articulated so far, it is clear that there is no ready answer to the way Christian Churches have responded, or are responding, to crises in Africa. We may pose a more fundamental question whether Christian Churches understand and appreciate Africa's crises from the perspective of Africans. To this question, the correct answer can only be that some Christians do, indeed. Historical evidence *prevents* us from affirming that Christian Churches (in general) have displayed such an understanding.

It remains paradoxically puzzling that although the Christian faith proclaims the Good News of total liberation (Isaiah 61:1–2; Luke 4:16–22); some of the missionary denominations have even offered a theological justification for colonialism. How can a theology of oppression and exploitation be compatible with the Gospel? How can a theology of racism and militarism be compatible with the Gospel of Jesus Christ? To those who are racially, culturally, economically or militarily oppressed, the Good News can only be that which proclaims liberation both historically and eternally — because history is absorbed in eternity.

The failure of the modern missionary enterprise (as a movement) to identify its activities with anti-colonial struggles led many committed African Christians to break away from missionary Christianity and establish movements which are compatible with the aspiration towards total liberation. Thus the rise of Independent African Christian Churches may be viewed as the logical consequence of the failure of the modern missionary enterprise to support the aspirations of African peoples. It is remarkable, in this connection, that the largest numbers of such Churches are to be found in South Africa, Zimbabwe and Kenya. A study of the colonial history of these countries, and of the attitudes of missionary denominations during the colonial period, shows that many Africans were disappointed with the missionary enterprise and enchanted by the Gospel of Jesus Christ.[5]

As individuals, some Christian missionaries have identified themselves with the victims of oppression, exploitation and enslavement. Such individuals as Bartholome de las Casas are rare in Church history, but they punctuate that history with exceptions which make it impossible for opponents of the Gospel to impose a wholesome condemnation on the Church. The Programme of the World Council of Churches to Combat Racism has been heavily criticized by pious Christians in Europe and North America, but from the perspective of the victims of racism, that programme has demonstrated in action, more than words, what it means to be the Church in situations gripped by crises of racial brutality.

'Not every one who says to me, "Lord, Lord", shall enter the Kingdom of Heaven, but he who does the will of my Father who is in heaven. On that day, many will say to me, "Lord, Lord, did we not prophesy in your name, and cast out demons in your name, and do many mighty works in your name?" And will I declare to them, "I never knew you; depart from me you evildoers"' (Matt. 7:21–23 ff; cf, Matt. 25:14–31 RSV).

The challenge expressed categorically by Jesus in this text is addressed to all Christians, irrespective of their race, culture, rank or status. We all have to measure our faith and practice against this challenge. The responses of Christian Churches to crises in Africa have to be viewed, necessarily, in terms of what they *do* in critical situations. It is *not* what Christian Churches *preach,* that counts, but what they actually *do,* that bears witness to our commitment as Christians.

One question that needs to be answered as we get involved in dealing with crises is whether we are eliminating *causes,* or softening the symptoms. The softening of symptoms deepens the crisis by entrenching the causes. Too often in Africa, Christian Churches have tended to concentrate on First Aid and Relief Work, without dealing with the causes that produce destitution. It is Christian responsibility to deal primarily with the symptoms of the various crises which Africa is in. Only by eliminating the causes will Africa live beyond the crises of survival. Christian Churches (as movements) and Christians (as individual believers) can contribute a great deal in this endeavour. Each Church, each Christian movement and each Christian individual, must decide what the appropriate contribution will be. God is the ultimate judge of us all, and we are participants in a divine drama geared towards the humanization of those who are dehumanized.

NOTES

1. Matt. 16:18, 18:17.

2. John 18:36.

3. John 18:38.

4. Matt. 7: 1–5.

5. This point is clearly illustrated in David B. Barrett, *Schims and Renewal in Africa,* London: Oxford University Press, 1968. Also, Bengt Sundkler, *The Christian Ministry in Africa,* Paperback Edition, London: SCM, 1962; T.A. Beetham, *Christianity and the New Africa,* London: Pall Mall Press, 1967.

Chapter Five

NEW ORIENTATIONS IN THE ECUMENICAL SHARING OF RESOURCES

Introduction

The need for rethinking on the Ecumenical Sharing of Resources is occasioned by the fact that new circumstances have emerged which render obsolete, most of the assumptions on which the current sharing of resources in the Ecumenical Movement is based. This chapter does not present an exhaustive treatment of the issues at stake. Rather, suggestions are made which might pave the way for new strategies to make the Churches more relevant in a wide variety of contexts in the world today. The suggestions include the roles of both donors and recipients, as well as the mutual exchange of personnel and consultancy.

Historical Background

Ecumenism today does not have the same meaning it had in the first century of the Christian era. At that time, Christians were a persecuted and overlooked minority, whose activities and beliefs were popularly considered to be on the periphery of recognized religion and culture. In the Graeco-Roman society of the first century AD, religious traditions other than Christianity were considered more significant and important. After all, Christianity had not yet established a tradition.[1]

Nevertheless, the patterns of sharing resources began to emerge and crystallize and we have documented evidence of such ecumenical sharing in the New Testament. Acts 11:27–30 records one clear example of a concerted effort on the part of Christians in Antioch and other parts of Asia Minor, to send relief to Jerusalem and the resources that were shared included materials (food), personnel (Saul and Barnabas) and ideas (consultancy). The latter two aspects of resource sharing are emphasized again in Acts, chapter 13.

The drama of conflict, confrontation and synthesis in the book of the Acts is very instructive of our situation in this last quarter of the 20th century. In the "traditional" countries of Western Europe, there are some Christians who take a position similar to the one taken by the Pharisaic Jews as in Acts 15:1-5. The latter believe that they are the "true" followers of Christianity by "virtue" of belonging to particular prestigious countries or denominations. They think that the peoples of Africa, Asia and Latin America must be "circumcised" into European Culture before being recognized as Christians.[2]

At the same time, there are, in those countries of Europe, the missionary-minded Christians who follow the example of Barnabas and Saul. They are open and willing to recognize that the Spirit of God cannot be contained, controlled or directed by any man or woman — only God chooses where, how and in whom the Spirit will move (John 3:8).[3]

The division of Christendom into Eastern Orthodoxy and Western Catholicism altered the meaning of ecclesial ecumenism, because in practice there emerged two ecclesiastical worlds rather than one. The Ecumenical Sharing of Resources from the Council of Nicea (AD 325) until the Council of Trent (AD 1545 – 1563) was done in the context of two Oikoumenes — the Catholic West and the Orthodox East — which included the Churches of Egypt and Ethiopia.[4]

The Council of Trent recognized divisions within the Western Catholicism, with its centre of authority vested in the Bishop of Rome who was also primate of the whole Catholic Church. The teaching of Martin Luther was condemned and the Reformation movement was declared anathema. Nevertheless the Reformation gained momentum, and contributed significantly towards the emergence of nationalism in Europe. The settlement of the Americas by Europeans is largely due to the Reformation and Counter-Reformation in Europe. The introduction and establishment of Christianity in Africa and Asia is also due to the Reformation and Counter-Reformation. Thus we note the emergence of three Oikoumenes in Europe during the sixteenth and seventeeth centuries: the Orthodox Oikoumene, the Catholic Oikoumene and the Protestant Oikoumene. The Ecumenical Sharing of Resources could not cross the structural boundaries of these

Oikoumenes, because there was neither mutual respect nor mutual recognition.

The Modern Christian Missionary Enterprise which accelerated towards the end of the nineteeth century and throughout the twentieth, facilitated the emergence of a fourth Oikoumene, comprising the new Churches of Africa, Asia, and Latin America (AALA).[5] It is undeniable that a New Reformation has occurred in the twentieth century and that this Reformation is still in process. The World Missionary Conference (Edinburgh, 1910), is the milestone which marks the beginning of this New Reformation. Other milestones can be mentioned, such as the International Missionary Conference at Tambarama near Madras in 1938; the Third WCC Assembly in 1961; the Second Vatican Council in 1962 – 1965, the Fourth Assembly of the WCC at Uppsala in 1968, the Fifth Assembly of the WCC at Nairobi in 1975, and the Faith and Order Conference at Lima, Peru, in 1982. Each of these milestones is cited here because of the uniqueness of the perspectives that characterized the deliberations thereof.[6]

Time and space do not permit a full explanation of the significance of these conferences as milestones of the New Reformation. Let it suffice to observe that the Old Christendom has almost become overshadowed by new forms of Christianity in Africa, Asia, and Latin America. In Europe and North America today, there is anxiety and concern that the Foundations of Protestantism and Catholicism are being shaken by new hermeneutics and new ecclesiology, evolved in the cultural and historical contexts of Africa, Asia and Latin America. It is instructive for all of us who profess the Christian faith to appreciate that this phenomenon — the phenomenon of Reformation — is inevitable, necessary and healthy, for it reminds us of the imperfection and finitude of human efforts.

The Modern Ecumenical Movement since the Vatican II has tended towards convergence, despite efforts to undermine the rapprochement between Protestantism, Catholicism and Orthodoxy. During this period, the Christians of Africa, Asia and Latin America have been lured towards one or other of the three Oikoumenes, but they have found it inappropriate to identify fully with any camp. Whenever necessary, they have identified with their confessional "parents," but they have not felt fully bound to those "families" after 'coming of age.' This new situation, in which the former mission stations have become full-grown churches with their own missionary outreach, calls for an entirely new orientation in the ecumenical sharing of resources.

The New Ecumenical Arena

The racing track in the new ecumenical arena was demarcated in 1961, when the International Missionary Council was integrated into the World Council of Churches as the Division of World Mission and Evangelism. From a theological perspective, this integration represented a major shift in the theology of the Christian Mission. In retrospect, it seems ridiculous that Christian mission was conducted in autonomy and isolation from the total life of the Church. A missionary society which functions autonomously and in isolation from the sponsoring church is deficient, for it lacks sacramental and ecclesial wholeness.

Conversely, a Church which delegates its missionary responsibility to a voluntary autonomous society, fails to take its mission seriously for while the mission is the only *raison d'etre'* for any Christian Community, it is not an optional luxury, but the core of ecclesiastical vocation. The realization of these theological insights was expressed as early as 1937, when proposals were made for the establishment of a World Council of Churches to serve as an ecumenical forum for all members. However, the full implementation did not come until 1961, when the World Council of Churches was launched in 1948. The lag of the thirteen years between 1948 and 1961 made some missionary-minded ecumenists comfortable in the older theology of Christian Mission, which separated the Church from its missionary calling. When the WCC Third Assembly at New Delhi finally resolved to incorporate Mission with *Church,* the advocates of the older view were very disturbed. One of the lines of criticism against the World Council of Churches hammers on this integration of the Church with its call to Mission. The World Council of Churches, however, has since 1961 taken the view that mission is an integral part of the life of the Church and not a special assignment set aside for autonomous para-church and pseudo-ecumenical organizations.

The Second Vatican Council introduced a new dimension in ecumenical relations when Pope John XXIII lifted the anathema imposed on Protestants since the Council of Trent in the sixteenth century. Catholics were allowed to interact with Protestants, and even with non-Christians. In recognition of the changed circumstances in the contemporary world since that time, relationships between Catholics and Protestants have improved considerably. There are some Christians, however, who do not appreciate the positive transformation and continue to wish that antagonism would continue. Conflicts during the Reformation and Counter-Reformation were exploited in the course of cultivating modern European nationalism. What would be the advantage of perpetuating those conflicts in Africa, Asia and Latin America? It has been expressed many times in the Ecumenical Association of Third World Theologians (EATWOT) that such conflicts are obsolete and irrelevant for our time.[7]

The third factor in our contemporary situation is the emergence of new, constitutionally independent nations in Africa, Asia and Latin America. Most of the countries in those regions were colonies of European powers, and became independent nations in the 1950s and 1960s. Their new constitutional status, with only a few exceptions, was 'negotiated' with the former colonial masters in order to prevent a deadlock which as in South Africa would have perpetuated bloodshed. Nationalism in Europe was not negotiated between colonial masters and colonial subjects. It was carved out of collapsing empires whose rulers could no longer wield effective power. European tribal and religious wars were fought, but these were for settling boundaries and clarifying the chain of command in Europe. Within our contemporary situation, the former colonial masters have continued to maintain economic dominance that was assured at the negotiated settlements.

The challenge for the Churches of former colonial masters has been to define the new relationships with the Churches of the former colonial subjects in such a way that the Gospel is indeed manifested as Good News.

During the colonial period, the Christian Missionary Enterprise was bad news to many colonial subjects, because some missionaries did not show themselves to be supportive of the struggle against colonial domination. The failure to support the struggle for humanization continues to be a scandal to the Gospel of Jesus Christ. The Ecumenical Movement has had to face the challenge of seeking new patterns of a relationship which would genuinely review the past in order to learn from mistakes and improve on the future. During the 1960s and 1970s, the patterns of ecumenical sharing of resources were largely a continuation of the unbalanced structures established in the colonial period. For example, the ecumenical sharing of personnel could not be carried out equitably since advanced theological education was denied African Church leaders during the colonial period.

Nor could there be an equitable, or balanced sharing of financial resources, since the countries of Africa were designed to be producers of raw materials and consumers of manufactured and processed goods. The consequence was that personnel and financial aid continued to flow from Europe and North America. Controversial discussions concerning the unbalanced flow of resources continued throughout the 1970s and 1980s. At the WCC Fifth Assembly (Nairobi, 1975), new patterns of sharing were called for but, as yet, no clear orientations have emerged. In the meantime, the steam generated by the Moratorium Debate in the 1970s has driven a new engine, bypassing the three major ecclesial families and seeking new proselytes in Africa, Asia and Latin America.

This new engine bears the label of missionary activity, but its coaches carry various kinds of cargo and passengers with a variety of interests. Some are **Bible-toting missionaries**, others are crusaders against African culture in the name of (Western) civilization, yet others are crusaders against "Communism" in the name of "freedom". The noise of the new engine has not sounded good news despite the proclamation of its heralds.

Good News is self-proclaiming. One does not need to be told that some information is good news if indeed it is Good News. For example, how are people in Africa expected to respond when they are told that a good harvest in USA is bad news for the farmers here? A good harvest is Good News in Africa because it means there is food. But it is bad news to those who want high prices for the food they sell! The new engine is built on the profits accruing from the raw materials which are exported to Europe and North America at throwaway prices, owing to the prevailing international economic order. It is also based on the huge interests charged on national debts that can hardly be repaid.

Towards New Orientations in the Ecumenical Sharing of Resources

In view of the observations we have just made, how can the Modern Ecumenical Movement in general and the World Council of Churches in particular, pioneer new orientations in the sharing of resources? The following are some sketchy recommendations, each of which requires further deliberation and refining.

A. Sharing of Personnel

(i) *Training of high-level manpower*
Until now, the Scholarship programme of the WCC has concentrated on relatively low-level manpower training, although a few doctoral scholarships have been available. High-level manpower does not necessarily refer to doctoral theological studies — rather, it refers to the highest possible level of professional training. Only people with such

training can have the knowledge, skills, experience, competence and confidence to invent and innovate for the improvements needed in Africa, Asia and Latin America.

(ii)   *Building Confidence through Mutual Exchange*
The mutual exchange of personnel of equal calibre will help to build confidence and competence. Until now, it has been suggested in some quarters that Europe and North America are "Mission Fields" in need of evangelization. Some Churches have sent African "Missionaries" to Europe and North America. But alas! The funds for travel and accommodation have been paid by the receiving Churches. At the same time, the general education level of those who have been sent has been very low in comparison to the average level of education in those countries. What kind of mission is this?

It would be mutually enriching if persons of comparable education, age and experience were to exchange roles for specific periods, with preparation and follow-up. Such exchange would have the effect of correcting the distorted impressions presented by the mass media and organs of ideological propaganda.

(iii)   *Orientation of Visitors*
Before visitors come to Africa and Asia, they need a proper orientation, both in their countries of origin and in the countries they visit. The impressions inculcated by the mass media ought to be corrected if visitors are to benefit from short visits. Such orientation could be done by organizing programmed orientation courses in two parts, one in Europe (or North America) and one in Africa (or Asia or Latin America). For visitors to Europe and North America, the orientation process would be reversed.

There ought to be follow-up programmes for visitors to share critically their experiences with the people they left at home. Only a few people have the privilege of leaving their countries to go abroad. Those who have this privilege have an obligation to serve as the "windows" through which other people can "see" and "experience" the world. The Churches ought to facilitate such an educational process, with honesty.

(iv)   *Mutual Consultancy*
Consultancy is one of the most expensive services in the world today. When it is offered by experts from Europe and North America to governments and organizations in Africa, Asia and Latin America, the

latter have to pay dearly for it. Yet, when the experts from Africa, Asia, and Latin America offer the same services, they are not renumerated or acknowledged equally. This situation prevails even in theological colleges.

The Ecumenical Movement can build a pool of international consultants who are mutually respected and recognized for their knowledge, skill, competence and experience, and the renumeration should be even.

It has often been embarrassing to learn that "experts" who are less than half as qualified are having their salaries "topped-up" when they come to work in Africa, yet when qualified persons go to Europe and North America, a similar adjustment does not occur.

While it is true that such situations are rather rare, the Churches ought to set precedents which other agencies can emulate.

Research and Development

It is a well-known fact that practically all research and development on the basis of which the contemporary world is organized and managed is conducted in Europe and North America. Those stations of research and development which exist elsewhere are linked to the headquarters in the North.

Patents and copyrights are registered in Europe and North America leading to a situation in which all intellectual property in the world is monopolized in the North.

The Ecumenical Movement can facilitate a reversal or balancing of this situation by enabling local researchers in the South to conduct research and develop their inventions and innovations. It can be expected that such research will be very basic, since the data base is practically non-existent in the South. Nevertheless, it is the *principle* involved that is of greater importance here, not the quantity of aid.

Those who claim to be seriously concerned to help Africa, Asia, and Latin America ought to enable the intellectually talented citizens of those continents to contribute to the international pool of knowledge, without becoming additional drops in the river of the brain drain to the North. The programme on the ecumenical sharing of resources in the World Council of Churches can contribute towards the reversal of the brain-drain. It is not ironical that appropriate technology is researched in the North.

B.   Sharing of Information and Knowledge

The exchange of data, information and knowledge is perhaps one of the greatest shortcomings in the organizational structure of the Ecumenical Movement. The link between international ecumenical organizations and individual Christians is often quite remote, if not non-existent. This is especially the case in Africa, where literacy rates are low. The situation is especially alarming when one notices that even the clergy in Churches that are members of the WCC hardly know of what is going on in the Ecumenical Movement.

One way of overcoming this difficulty is for the Ecumenical Movement, through the National Councils of Churches, to promote the publication of well-documented books and journals, which would circulate both nationally and internationally. The *Ecumenical Review* and the *International Review of Mission* have served a very useful role in the history of the Ecumenical Movement.

This experience can be shared regionally and nationally. In Asia, it is already happening and it is not difficult to see it happening in Africa too.

The same would apply to the local development of the electronic media, although this requires a greater capital outlay and more careful planning and management.

C.   Collaboration with Government and Parastatal Organizations

It is becoming increasingly clear that Churches cannot carry out their planned projects without the support of the governments in countries where they operate. Conversely, with co-operation between religious and governmental organizations a great deal can be achieved.

The WCC Programme on the ecumenical sharing of resources can explore new ways of operating with governmental and parastatal organizations, without compromising the theological principles on which the Ecumenical Movement is founded. Such co-operation could, for example, be organized at the following levels:

(i)	Universities	— in postgraduate studies
		— specialized training
		— Research and Development Projects
(ii)	Health Programmes	— Immunization
		— Primary Health Care
		— Research

(iii) Agricultural Programmes — Research and Development

(iv) Energy and Environment — Especially in the promotin of projects which enhance environment and eliminate dependence.

Conclusion

These suggestions can be expanded to fill a lengthy volume. It is hoped, however, that enough creative ideas have been outlined which will help the reader to think of other ways of dealing with the problem at hand.

Certainly, the time is overdue for a review of many aspects of the Modern Ecumenical Movement. As we prepare to enter the twenty-first century, it will be worthwhile to ask ourselves what insights we are bequeathing to the next generation. In the seventeenth century, Isaac Newton bequeathed fixed natural laws; in the twentieth century, Albert Einstein bequeathed the theory of Relativity.

Immanuel Kant in the 18th century and Dietrich Bonhoeffer in the twentieth, both thought that humanity had come of age. As the twentieth century draws to a close and the twenty-first ushers in, it appears that humanity is only entering adolescence, with a great deal of juvenile delinquency. Otherwise, how do we justify the arms race, the wanton environmental destruction and the unabated abuse of life? Hopefully, God will help us to grow towards responsible maturity in the twenty first-century. May the programme on the ecumenical sharing of resources help us to grow in the new orientation.

NOTES

1. For the cultural and religious setting of apostolic Christianity, see Paul Tillich, *A History of Christian Thought,* New York: Simon and Schuster, 1967, 1968. Also, Rudolf Bultmann, *Primitive Christianity in its Contemporary Setting,* London/Glasgow: Collins/Fontana, 1956.

2. This point has been discussed extensively in J.N.K. Mugambi, *The African Heritage and Contemporary Christianity,* Nairobi: Longman, 1989.

3. See, for example, Lesslie Newbigin, *Honest Religion For Secular Man,* London: SCM Press, 1964.

4. Philip Hughes, *The Church in crisis: A History of Twenty Great Councils,* London: Burns and Oates. Also, several relevant chapters in *History's Lessons for Tomorrow's Mission, op.cit.*

5. I prefer this geographically descriptive label, AALA, to the popularized and highly emotive terms, 'Third World' and 'The South'. The other cluster, according to the new labels, is ENA (Europe and North America). These are precise and sufficiently descriptive labels which are emotively neutral.

6. When historians investigated the events of the fifteenth and sixteenth centuries which characterize the Reformation, they may not appreciate that the reformers were not always conscious of being engulfed in a social movement. The interrelationship of these events became clearly evident only after the consequences of the reformers' campaigns. Likewise, future generations are likely to view the twentieth century as a period of a second Reformation in Church History. The Modern Ecumenical Movement is perhaps the most conspicuous aspect of this new Reformation. a comprehensive history of the Movement is not available, because it is still evolving in the context of new circumstances and challenges. Documents relating to various concerns of the Movement are obtainable from the WCC publications office in Geneva, which freely supplies its catalogues periodically.

7. See, for example, Sergio Torres, Opening Address to the Pan-African Conference of Third World Theologians, December 17–23, Accra, Ghana, in *African Theology en Route,* ed. Kofi Appiah-Kubi and Sergio Torres, New York: Orbis Books, 1979, pp. 3–9.

Chapter Six

SOME PROBLEMS OF CHRISTIAN THEOLOGICAL EDUCATION IN AFRICA

Introduction

Theology may be defined as the systematic articulation of man's response to revelation in particular contexts. It is the rationalization and justification of religious beliefs, teachings and practices. Theology is indispensable to every religion. Theological education is the institutionalized process through which the theologians of a particular religion are trained. In the present chapter we are concerned with Christian theological education.

Religious education in general serves as a starting point for theological education. Thus the teaching of Christian Religious Education in Kenya schools and colleges provides a foundation upon which prospective theology students can build their training. However, a clear distinction must be made between Christian *Religious* Education (which is general and introductory), and Christian *Theological* Education (which is detailed and specialized).[2]

The problems of Christian theological education in Africa may be discussed under several broad categories.[3] This chapter presents these problems under the following categories:

(i)   Resources;
(ii)   Conceptual tools;
(iii)   Analysis and Synthesis;
(iv)   Application;
(v)   **Curriculum Development.**

These categories have been arbitrarily listed for the purpose of discussion. It would be possible to recognize and reformulate the problems in a variety of ways. The most important point is that some theoretical framework is needed to facilitate discussion on such a wide topic as this.

Problems of Resources

The development of Christian Theological Education requires resources and facilities that are relevant to the needs of the Churches in Africa. Resources may be discussed under the following topics:

(i) *Personnel:* An educational process depends for its success on the availability of trained manpower in sufficient numbers to cope adequately with the demand. One of the major problems of Christian theological education in Africa, especially among the non-Catholic denominations, is the lack of adequately trained personnel to train theologians to cope relevantly with the needs of the Churches in Africa. Theological Colleges, Seminaries and Bible Schools in Africa are having to rely on expatriates for the task of theological formation. These expartriates will have been trained in cultural environments and intellectual traditions different from those of the students they come to teach. Consequently, the free exchange of ideas which is necessary in theological formation is hampered by cross-cultural barriers.

This problem of personnel seems to be a vicious circle. Why has it taken so long for the Churches in Africa to Africanize the teaching personnel in their Theological Colleges, Seminaries and Bible Schools? Several answers can be proposed in response to this question. One is that some African Church leaders have often preferred to engage expatriates rather than African teachers. Another is that many of the African theologians who are trained to work as theological educators are not retained by the Churches. Instead, they opt to work in secular institutions where they can obtain more appreciable remuneration.

To this point we shall return later. For the moment it is worthwhile to consider whether Christian Churches in Africa can conduct relevant and effective theological education without the total Africanization of the educators in the theological institutions. 'Africanization' in this context refers to the process whereby the curriculum is designed, developed, taught and evaluated by Africans themselves. Surely, the selfhood of any Church can be determined by the degree to which it is capable of maintaining its own process of theological formation!

(ii)   *The Working Environment:* In addition to personnel, the development of theological education requires an environment which promotes such development. Theologians need opportunities to discuss freely among themselves. They need library facilities to whet their intellect and update their knowledge. They also need outlets through which they can publish their ideas. Such facilities would encourage the older generation of theologians and prepare the younger generation. In contemporary Africa, Christian theologians have to do their work under very limiting and limited environments, often unconductive to theological creativity. The theologians are often overloaded and overworked, and they can hardly afford to buy books and theological journals to enhance their work. Consequently, much of their work tends to become routine instruction, preparing their students more to counsel than to do theology. Professor J.S. Mbiti has remarked that the Churches in Africa have yet to develop their theological identity. They have already come into being numerically, but they have some way to go before they come into being theologically.

Roland Oliver has also observed that the Churches in Africa face the risk of "expanding at the circumference while disintegrating at the centre". By this he means that most African Churches have not developed their theological infrastructures with as much vigour as they have welcomed new converts. The theological dimension of our Churches can best be nurtured through the adoption of measures that promote, for theologians, a working environment conducive to theological productivity. Some denominations have established publishing houses, bookshops and research centres. These measures should be encouraged. In addition, theologians need grants to enable them purchase books, conduct research, organize conferences and publish their findings. The Ecumenical Movement can greatly enhance the development of a favourable working environment for theologians. However, each Church will have to support and sponsor any ecumenical initiatives, as a necessary measure to prevent paternalism and expatriate interference.

(iii)   *Training and Retaining:* Closely related to the problems concerning the working environment are problems of training and retaining theological personnel. We have already noted that personnel is one of the major problems in the development of theological education in Africa. Training is expensive. It takes a long time and the drop-out rate increases with every increase in the level of specialization. Thus only very few of those who join the Bible Schools and theological colleges end up as professional theologians.

The problem here is that the very few theologians who qualify at the highest levels of training are often not retained by the respective Churches. Sometimes the promising students who have determination, interest and aptitude are not given encouragement and support by their Churches. So they undertake studies at their own expense and, on completion, they take their own initiatives to seek employment. It is important for our Churches to ensure that they train and retain the best possible theologians. This can be done by establishing training programmes and the terms of services which attract people who would otherwise have been engaged elsewhere. While it is true that material and financial considerations should not be the main factors to determine admission, it is also true that such considerations should be taken seriously. "Man shall not live by bread *alone*", but *bread* is important nonetheless.

(iv)   *Language:* Schooling in the countries South of the Sahara is conducted in languages that are culturally foreign to the peoples living in those areas. These foreign languages are English, French and Portuguese. The majority of people in those areas do not speak or even understand these languages. Thus education in general, and theological training in particular, are conducted in languages that are foreign to both the African theologians and to the majority of the African Christian congregations. How can African Christian theologians promote the relevant theological education in foreign languages? The problem of language is complex, and Christian Churches may not resolve it in isolation from the policies of governments. It is true that the ethnic plurality in African countries makes it difficult for Churches to promote the use of local languages.

However, it seems to me logical and practical to adopt a policy in which theological education is conducted in the same language as preaching and pastoral care. In East Africa, especially in Kenya, a rather interesting multi-lingualism is evolving. Schooling and office administration are conducted in English. Commerce and national politics are conducted in Kiswahili, which is also the common language in urban centres. The local languages are used at home, for socialization of children and for the inculcation of culture. For many people in East Africa, English is a third or fourth language, after one or two local languages and Kiswahili, which is the *lingua franca* of the region. Yet most theological writing that has been published in East Africa is written in English. The problem of language needs thorough investigation as a factor limiting effective theological Education in Africa.

(v)   *Confidence:* African theologians need to have confidence in themselves. The colonial legacy has lingered on for a long time, and many Africans continue to consider themselves incapable of originality, creativity and inventiveness. Within our Churches, it is necessary to promote an attitude of self-confidence, so that African Christians can consider themselves as fellows in mission, together with Christians from other parts of the world. Africans may be financially handicapped, but they are not less human because of their financial poverty. African Christian theologians need opportunities to meet and exchange ideas with one another in conferences, seminars, workshops and consultations. Such opportunities will help to build this confidence and provide exposure for the participants. It is through such interactions that convergence will emerge between the many perspectives held by various theologians.

Conceptual Problems

The conceptual tools with which African Christian theologians have to work have been developed in alien cultural traditions. Not only are African theologians expected to express themselves in foreign languages; they are also expected to base their theology on concepts that were developed in the context of an intellectual tradition that is rather remote from the African heritage.

It seems that one valuable approach for African theological educators would be to encourage discussion about the debates that led to the doctrines now accepted as central to the Christian faith. What, for instance, would be the African contributions to the Christian doctrines of God, salvation, eschatology, the Church, Christology, and so on? These concepts continue to be debated about by theologians in Europe and North America. Theological education in Africa needs to prepare the younger students of theology to participate, with originality and creativity, in discussions concerning such central concepts.

The teaching of philosophy can be very useful in such preparation. For a long time now, the Catholic Church has required of its seminarians to study philosophy before embarking on theological studies. Philosophy is considered a prerequisite for theological formation. It appears that some Protestant denominations are reluctant to incorporate philosophy in their programme of theological training. This reluctance is perhaps due to the fear that philosophically trained theologians might be too critical. However, the long-established practice in the Catholic Church shows that philosophy does not destroy faith. Rather, it can greatly strengthen it by building strong foundations for belief and for apologetics.

Conceptually, theological education in Africa can also be greatly enhanced if an inter-disciplinary approach is adopted. Again, Protestants may learn from the Catholic Church in this respect. Our Churches may adopt a policy whereby theological education would involve training in a "secular" profession before the student enters the seminary, or enters the seminary at the same time as he studies for "secular" subjects. Such a system would help the seminarians to benefit from the "secular" disciplines through interaction. At the same time, the students of theology might be able to contribute theologically in the secular disciplines or professions in which they relate and work.

Problems of Analysis and Synthesis

Theological Education in Africa has followed the analysis and synthesis developed in and for North-Atlantic theological institutions. The theology curriculum has remained rather fixed and compartmentalized. Biblical studies have been divided into Old Testament and New Testament specializations. Systematics and Dogmatics have been separated. Christian Ethics and Pastoral Studies have again been compartmentalized.

The integration of the theology curriculum might follow a different orbit if the needs of African Churches were reviewed. This task calls for the involvement of African theologians, particularly those who have been locally trained and have managed to display originality and creativity. This, of course, is not to imply that foreign-trained African theologians should not be involved. Many of our theologians who have been trained abroad are very conscious (sometimes over-conscious) of the prejudices inculcated in them during their training. The review of the theology curriculum needs to be based on insights from all quarters. To this point we shall return shortly.

Problems of Application

Theological Education in Africa needs to be relevant and applicable. One of the shortcomings of the present process of theological formation is that much of what students study at college is neither relevant nor applicable to the situations in the parishes and institutions where they go to work after completing their training. Thus the students have to learn on the job, despite their training.

To meet the need for relevance and applicability, the structure of theological education may have to be reviewed. More practical work, seminars, visits to parishes and other operational areas, guest-speaker programmes and so on, may have to be introduced. The period of training may have to be prolonged, while improving the quality and raising the certification levels. It is already past time for theological colleges in Africa to introduce degree programmes including masters, doctoral and post-doctoral training. It may appear too ambitious to suggest this now, but surely, African Churches have to take the decision now if they expect to accomplish these objectives within a decade. The sooner the policy decision is made the earlier the planning process will begin, and the sooner the objective will be achieved. For how long will African Churches continue to rely on foreign institutions for the training and certification of high-calibre personnel? Only by designing and implementing such programmes will African Churches become theologically self-reliant.

Problems of Curriculum Development

Theological education in Africa will need to be organized in accordance with the most up-to-date educational principles. Thus the development of theological curriculum will need to be done through the involvement of professional educators who are familiar with, and sympathetic to, the needs of the Churches.

Curriculum development is a professional undertaking which should be conducted by professionals. The Churches in Africa have many professional educators in their membership who may not be theologians. If such educators were invited to formulate appropriate curricula in collaboration with theologians and other Church personnel, we might evolve theological programmes that are professionally sound and theologically effective.

Curriculum development involves not only the formulation of syllabi, but also the provision of teaching materials and other resources. Though publishing is expensive, our Churches need to find ways of providing teaching materials at affordable prices. The Lutheran Theological Seminary in Tanzania has for many years published the *Africa Theological Journal,* which is a cumulative source of stimulating theological ideas. The Catholic Pastoral Institute for Eastern Africa in Eldoret, Kenya, has also produced several publications relevant to theological education in the region. Such creative ventures need to be encouraged and, whenever possible, Churches should engage in co-operative efforts, avoiding duplication and competition.

The Ecumenical Movement can help the Churches in Africa in the projects of curriculum development by responding to their requests, especially when such requests are made on a regional and co-operative basis.

Conclusion

The points raised above have not exhausted the topic we set out to discuss. They have, however, provided some issues for debate and comment. There has been no attempt to give conclusive solutions to any of the problems. Workable solutions can be reached only after lengthy discussion. If what has been presented has stimulated the reader to think of solutions or to reformulate any of the problems in new ways, the author will have achieved one of the objectives that motivated this chapter.

NOTES

1. Paul Tillich, *Systematic Theology,* Vol. I, University of Chicago Press, 1951, Introduction.

2. Religious Education is normally provided at the pre-primary, primary and secondary levels of the public school curriculum, whereas theological education is the specialization of seminaries and University faculties of theology. Effective theological training demands well qualified teachers, well equipped libraries, standard admission and examination procedures, as well as a studious and reflective environment. This chapter is intended to outline some of the problems related to these requirements.

3. In the 1970s the Theological Education Fund sponsored an Evaluation of Theological Education programmes in Africa, Asia and Latin America. The report of that evaluation used a different set of categories, but in general agrees with the substance of this chapter. See also, Paul Miller, *Equipping for Ministry in East Africa,* Dodoma: Central Tanganyika Press, 1969. Also, Herbert M. Zorn, *Viability in Context: A Study of the Financial Viability of Theological Education in the Third World — Seedbed or Sheltered Garden?* Bromley, Kent: Theological Education Fund, 1975.

Chapter Seven

THE SOCIAL CONTEXT OF CHRISTIANITY IN COLONIAL AND POST-COLONIAL AFRICA

Graeco-Roman Colonialism in Africa

The Roman Province of Africa was founded in 146 BC following the destruction of Carthage by Roman legions. Alexander the Great had occupied Egypt nearly two hundred years previously, and established in 323 BC the beginning of Egyptian assimilation into Hellenic civilization. From that year onwards, Alexandria in Egypt became the intellectual centre of the Hellenic Oikoumene and was to continue occupying that status until its conquest by Islam during the seventh century of the Christian era.[1]

From the perspective of Europe, Africa consisted of the Egyptian and Carthaginian domains, which extended to all the areas on the southern shores of the Mediterranean Sea. Europeans did not know how far south Africa extended, and they were not interested in such knowledge since Carthage and Egypt provided the indirect link between tropical Africa and Europe.[2] It was not until the fifteenth century of the Christian era that Europe became interested in exploring the coasts of Africa, but even then, the exploration was only a means to an end. Portugal and Spain were interested in the search for alternative ocean routes to India and China and for this end the African coasts had to be explored.[3]

The Egyptians and Carthaginians had prosperous commercial and cultural contacts with tropical and equatorial Africa, dating from prehistoric times. Chancellor Williams in *The Destruction of Black Civilization* suggests that the cultural centre of ancient Egypt was in the Upper Nile, and that the gradual decline of Egypt was the result of prolonged pressure from the peoples of West Asia.[4] Jerome Carcopino has observed that the Roman emperors enjoyed the destruction of thousands of wild animals imported from Africa, including hippopotami from Nubia. In AD 80, for example, a total of five thousand beasts were killed on one day at the inauguration by Emperor Titus. of the Colosseum in Rome. On two separate days, respectively, 2,246 and 443 wild beasts were killed for the entertainment of Emperor Trajan (AD 52–117). These animals include hippopotami, lions, tigers and elephants.[5] The destruction of the environment of northern Africa, while facilitating the production of grain to feed southern Europe and Asia Minor, ensured the encroachment of the desert and the migration of the African peoples to the tropics. The whole of Africa South of the Sahara abounds with stories tracing many ethnic groups to northern Africa.[6]

The Graeco-Roman Africa covered the territory North of the Sahara, and in this region there settled many colonists from southern Europe marginalizing the indigenous inhabitants.[7] European settler colonialism in northern Africa was destroyed by Islamic expansion during the second half of the seventh century. The region did not, however, experience any more cultural and religious freedom under the Arabs than had been possible under Graeco-Roman colonists. Instead, the entire area was incorporated into the Arab-Islamic civilization that was sweeping westwards across northern Africa towards Portugal and Spain. Since the seventh century, northern Africa has remained an integral part of the Arab-Islamic Oikoumene.

The contribution of North African Christianity to Catholicism is remarkable. With Alexandria as the intellectual centre of Graeco-Roman civilization, it is not surprising that the most renowned Christian theologians of pre-Islamic times, were based in north Africa, even though they may not have been of African ancestry. S.C. Neill rightly notes that the Donatist Schism was not theological but also racial, linguistic, cultural and economic.[8]

The survival of Christianity in Egypt and Ethiopia, in spite of Islamic pressure to conform, is evidence of the deep-rootedness of the Christian faith in those areas. Interestingly, these Churches which survived the onslaught of Islam had already been declared heretical in the Ecumenical Councils of Nicea (AD 325) and Chalcedon (AD 451). Their refusal to submit to the pressures of Rome for structural conformity is further evidence of the transposition of Gospel in the cultural keys of the Egyptians and Ethiopians.[9]

The Reformation and Colonial Settlement in Africa

Contact between Europe and Africa South of the Sahara along the West Coast did not begin until the 15th Century, when Portugal and Spain were competing in search of alternative routes to India and China. The Portuguese, after several attempts, managed to sail around the southern cape and reached India early in 1498. However, the calling ports established by the Portuguese for resting, servicing and replenishing their ships, did not become centres of colonial settlement until much later. They were also to be among the last European strongholds in Africa.

The first planned European occupation of Africa South of the Sahara was in 1652, when some Puritans arrived at the southern cape running away from their countries in search of freedom.[10] Many of them were from Holland, which was then the most liberal of European countries. It is an ironical twist of history that those who invaded and established themselves at the southern tip of Africa in the name of religious freedom, were in fact running away from the liberalization of Europe as a result of the Reformation. If they felt persecuted in Europe, it is ironical that they became oppressors in Africa. Their claim to the Christian faith is an embarrassment in Church history, which makes many Africans wonder whether the Gospel of Jesus is indeed a proclamation of total humanization and liberation. Fortunately, the scriptures rather than social institutions provide a standard against which the piety of individuals and organizations can be tested and challenged.

The puritans' experience of tribalism, sectarianism and intolerance in Europe was exported to Africa and maintained with their settlement, later on to be refined into the ghetto ideology of apartheid.

Apart from this settlement of religious fugitives at the southern cape, settler colonialism was not effected in the rest of Africa South of Sahara until the last quarter of the nineteenth century. The Berlin Conference on Colonial Questions, (1884–85) was convened by Bismark to ensure Germany's share in the scramble for and partition of Africa.[11] This Conference established the spheres of influence of the European nations who laid claim to colonies in Africa. The maps were drawn without any consultation with the African peoples or their leaders and yet, a century later, Africa has to endeavour to maintain these arbitrary territorial borders.

The Berlin Treaty included special provisions for the protection of missionary organizations and religious activities, but owing to the presence of Turkey as a participating and interested power, Christianity could not be explicitly mentioned. In spite of that protection, which was written into the treaty, most Christian missionary societies dared not venture into the territories where they could not be sure of protection. In practice, therefore, missionary societies tended to work in areas where their home governments were directly involved. This is how it happened that the layout of

Christianity in Africa South of the Sahara was patterned on the models operative in the respective metropolitan countries. If Catholicism was dominant in a European country, Catholicism would be dominant in its African colonies. Thus in all French colonies, Catholicism was dominant, whereas in all British colonies it was Anglicanism, while in all German colonies, Lutheranism prevailed until Germany was defeated in the two world wars. Even then, Lutheranism is more prevalent in former German colonies than anywhere else in Africa South of the Sahara.[12]

Christianity and the Slave Trade

In the period between the rise of Islam in the seventh century and the re-consolidation of Europe in the twentieth, Africans were subjected to the slave trade — first across the Indian Ocean and then across the Atlantic. During the Middle Ages, the institution of slavery was justified on Aristotelean, rather than Christian grounds. Just as Aristotle had approved of slavery, so did Thomas Aquinas (1224-74) and other schoolmen approve of it (or, rather, saw no point in opposing it).[13] The conquest and settlement of the Americas by European Christians was accompanied by the vicious trade in African slaves. It is strange that people who were running away from their home countries in search of freedom were to become traders in human cargo.

According to Aristotle, a slave was an "animated instrument" who was "nothing in himself".[14] This was the definition applied by the slave traders and slave owners across the Atlantic, until the Industrial Revolution replaced slave labour with automated production. Thus the Abolitionist Movement had more to do with economics and politics than with Christian doctrine.[15]

The teaching of the reformers, with its emphasis on scripture rather than tradition, should have provided the basis for the campaigns against the slave trade. However, such campaigns gained momentum in the late eighteenth century, not in the sixteenth and seventeenth when the Reformation was at its height. How is it that slavery and the slave trade escaped the attention of the reformers? How is it that the critics against Christianity were more outspoken against this evil than the Church? These contradictions have led Paul Johnson, in *Caution: God at Work,* to discuss the "tragic necessity of Karl Marx".[16] He suggests that Marx's criticism of religion would have been unnecessary if the Church had lived up to its biblical calling.

The rediscovery of the Bible did not yield a theology categorically committed to liberation. It was not until the 20th century, in reaction against the modern missionary enterprise, that theologies of liberation were explicitly articulated, first in the Americas, and later, all over the world.[17]

Between A.D. 1500 and 1800, Africa South of Sahara was related to Europe mainly as a source of cheap labour, which was also big business. For three hundred years, the Church was silent on the evil and, even when individual Christians began to speak out, they could only mobilize public opinion through voluntary societies unrelated to the institutional ecclesiastical structures.

The nineteenth century opened with several missionary societies already established for the purpose of evangelizing the peoples of Africa and Asia. These societies were to combine preaching with the abolition of the slave trade across the Indian Ocean. It is interesting, however, that the involvement of Christian missionary organizations in this project became co-ordinated and accentuated only after attention was directed to the Arab involvement. In the middle of the nineteenth century, Livingstone could campaign against the Arab slave trade in favour of British Christianity and "legitimate commerce". But John Wesley, one hundred years earlier, could not make slavery and slave trade major issues during his open-air preaching in Georgia, where the evil was rampant![18]

It has sometimes been argued that Africans themselves collaborated with the slave traders to perpetuate this evil. Such an argument, however, is a very weak justification. Africa's "chiefs" did not own any ships to transport slaves. They did not own any plantations to engage slaves across the Atlantic. They did not make guns and chains to enforce their interests. The attempt to apportion blame in this way fails from the start, just like the other distortion of history which portrays African peoples as "hostile" and "warlike" because of resisting European invasion. What ought they to have done?

The Modern Missionary Enterprise and Colonization of Africa

The effective colonization of Africa South of the Sahara by European nations is inextricably bound with the modern Christian Missionary Enterprise. Among the factors generally associated with the rise of the Modern Missionary Movement are the following:

(i)   Protestantism, which needed new converts outside Europe to counter-balance Catholicism.

(ii)   Evangelical revivals in Europe and North America, which motivated people to allocate resources for the further spread of Christianity.

(iii) Campaigns to abolish the slave trade, which necessitated the rehabilitation of the freed slaves.

(iv)   Increase in geographical knowledge, which made people in Europe and North America aware of the conditions in Africa, Asia and in the oceanic islands.

(v)   Improvement in transport and communications, which made travel and feedback easier.

(vi)   A new national consciousness, which gave many Europeans and North Americans sense of destiny as heralds of civilization. In this respect, European and American missionaries considered their work to be an integral part of their nationalist ideology. It is for this reason that most missionaries preferred to work in territories claimed and protected by their own colonial governments and armies.

(vii) The rise of secularism in Europe and North America, which made many evangelicals apprehensive about the future of Christianity and motivated them to evangelize other parts of the world before secularism became world-wide.

S.C. Neill has observed that four invading forces in Africa reinforced one another to produce an overwhelming impact, which was to permanently transform Africa.[19] *Explorers* paved the way, and satisfied their geographical curiosity. *Missionaries* followed, and established mission stations which were to become the centres of the invading culture, and points of contact with the colonial administration.

Most *missionaries* were satisfied with converting Africans to Christianity in order to save them from damnation in Hell. The *administrators,* however, were more interested in the social and political impact of missionary activity. If the missionaries could teach Africans to become obedient subjects, they could be assured of protection and even financial support from the colonial office. This happened, for instance, with regard to the educational work of British Missionary Societies in Kenya, which received substantial grants-in-aid.[20]

The *settlers* and *traders* could then exploit the resources (both human and natural) for the benefit of the industries in Europe and North America. Interestingly, many of the colonies in Africa South of the Sahara started as properties granted to chartered corporations which were expected to exploit the resources for maximum profit. Administrative and military presence would be for facilitating this process and missionary activity would be to prepare the population for the new era.

It would be a distortion of historical facts for anyone to dissociate the modern Christian missionary enterprise from the process of colonization in Africa South of the Sahara. What is required, after acknowledging this association, is to discern the lessons from that past, in the hope that they might help the Church to perform better at present and in the future. Without self-criticism, the Church cannot live up to the tasks for which it is meant to exist.[21]

Christianity and the Anti-Colonial Struggle

Despite the failures, weaknesses and shortcomings of the modern Christian Missionary Enterprise, the Gospel made a positive impact in Africa South of the Sahara. It is amazing that this happened, given the association that was evident or apparent between the explorers, missionaries, administrators and traders settlers. A relatively large number of Africans came to identify themselves as Christians, though the numbers attracted varied from place to place and from one missionary to another.

At the same time, many African Christians understood it to be their duty and obligation to struggle for their liberation against all forces of colonialism. Efforts by the missionary enterprise to dissociate the Gospel from socio-political concerns and give it another worldly emphasis did not succeed. How could it succeed when the missionaries themselves were in practice, cultural agents of their own nations? How could it succeed while the missionaries were teaching African students and catechists to be loyal and obedient to the imperial masters? In the face of such contradiction, most missionaries would reply: "Do as I say, but not as I do!" Such an answer would not suffice however, and, to most schooled Africans, missionary teaching lost credibility.

The authority of the resident missionary was replaced by that of the Bible. This was especially so after the scriptures became available in the African languages. David Barrett has observed that a schism against missionary institutions was more likely to occur where the Bible had been translated into an African language.[22]

It is interesting to note that this phenomenon occurred when Moses issued a new set of commandments as the standard to measure all theory and practice. The law became the basis of authority for the prophets who courageously challenged the kings and priests of Israel and Judah. This phenomenon repeated itself when Jesus in his public ministry, on the basis of the law of Moses, openly criticized the pietism of the Pharisees and of other elite groups in Palestine. The ordinary people were amazed at his teaching, for he taught them as one who had authority, not as their scribes (Matt. 7:28–29). Thus the credibility of the scribes was eroded, and replaced by the authority of Jesus.

Likewise, during the Reformation, the authority of the Church was replaced by that of the scriptures, even though Protestant institutionalism was to lead to further fragmentation of Protestant denominations. In the twentieth century, African Christians accepted the authority of Jesus and became Christians. In doing so, they bypassed missionary authority, associated as it was with colonialism and imperialism. The failure of the modern missionary enterprise to openly condemn and combat colonialism compromised the acceptability of missionaries to Africans, but it did not compromise the Gospel. Rather, African Christians became empowered by their conversion to struggle for their humanization and liberation. This situation has continued in South Africa.

Christianity and African Nationalism

When at last the decolonization of Africa became inevitable, the Church institutions established by the modern missionary enterprise found themselves in crisis. How would they be received by the governments of the new African nations? There was a great deal of apprehension in the late 1950s and early 1960s, concerning the future of Christianity in post-colonial Africa. It was feared that Christianity would be discarded together with the colonial relics. It has surprised many Europeans and North Americans that, instead of declining, Christianity has continued to grow after the attainment of constitutional independence in most African nations within the tropics.

The first country to achieve constitutional nationhood in tropical Africa was Ghana, formerly called Gold Coast (to emphasize its value for Europe). Under the leadership of Kwame Nkrumah, Ghana became a republic within the British Commonwealth in March 1957. The Modern Missionary Enterprise in Ghana had not identified itself with the struggle for national liberation in that country. Thus the political leadership did not consider Christian Churches to be a necessary component of the new nation. The Churches themselves were slow in adjusting themselves to the new situation, and took offence when Nkrumah declared that the search for political liberation was logically prior to the search and preparation for the "Kingdom of God". This new political creed was derived from practical experience in Ghana's struggle for national sovereignty, a struggle to which the missionary enterprise had rendered itself irrelevant.

The Churches could not tolerate their marginalization by the national political establishment. Conversely, the political establishment could not survive without the support of the Church. The consquence was that Ghana, as a young African nation, suffered a distabilization from which it has yet to recover. From a historical perspective, the Ghana case illustrates that the challenge is for the Church and the missionary enterprise to discern the signs of the times and to adjust quickly enough so as to be constructively useful and relevant in situations of rapid social change.

This experience of Ghana is illustrative of many contemporary situations in Africa. During the struggle for national sovereignty, the Churches, as social structures, have often refused or hesitated to side with nationalist aspirations. When finally the struggle was won,they found themselves marginalized and lost their previous social influence and prestige. They thus rendered themselves irrelevant by their failure to identify themselves directly with African nationalism.

It would be deceptive, in the twentieth century, for anyone to deny the centrality of national interests in all aspects of interaction between peoples. If Africans are nationalistic, it is because they are responding to the nationalist interests and pressures from other parts of the world. African Christianity will become irrelevant if it fails to reckon with this fact.

Christianity in Post-Colonial Africa

On the achievement of national sovereignty, each African country has had to define the role of religion as a social institution. The official position has depended on the specific history of the country concerned and the relative influence of the various religious groups within the nation-state. The role of various religious groups in the nationalist struggle is another variable. In Africa, North of the Sahara, Islam has been understood and appreciated as a unifying force, facilitating a nationalist struggle against Euro-American domination. South of the Sahara, both Protestantism and Catholicism have been suspected, owing to the apparent or evident reluctance of both local and expatriate leaders to openly identify themselves with African nationalist aspirations.

Ironically, Christian missionaries working in Africa are fully committed and loyal to their own governments, without question, but somehow they seem to expect their African counterparts to be disloyal to their own countries. These would appear to be double standards, which are not compatible with the Gospel because of their apparent hypocrisy.

As for the African Christians themselves, the process of adjustment has been rather long. The nature of this adjustment may not become clear until after two or more generations. At the time of writing, most African Christian Churches are still headed by leaders who took over from expatriate missionaries, or by successors chosen with the implicit or explicit approval of the parent denomination abroad.[23]

The African Charismatic Churches,[24] wherever they existed, had an important role during the struggle for national sovereignty, and were banned or suppressed by the colonial administrations. After the achievement of constitutional independence, the ban and restriction was lifted, but the Churches were not structurally equipped and ready for coping with the challenges of modern nation-building. For example, most of them did not have educational, medical and social structures which are necessary in contemporary national reconstruction. Their own leaders had a relatively low level of schooling. These limitations have made it difficult for those Churches to take a leading role in the new nations, even though they may have been supportive of the nationalist struggle. Sometimes, owing to a lack of awareness and exposure, they have come into conflict with the state.

A new wave of missionary organizations has invaded African countries after independence. These new organizations, mainly from Europe and North America, have taken advantage of the new constitutional guarantees to freedom of worship. Theoretically, their general aim is to evangelize, but in practice they introduce and induce the cultural values of the societies and nations which they represent. Unfortunately, most of those missionary and para-church organizations come to oppose and compete, rather than co-operate and collaborate with the older missionary organizations and mission-related Churches. Consequently, the new organizations risk repeating the same mistakes committed in the past and, in the long term, lose credibility when crucial choices have to be taken in matters of liberation. Division and confusion often result in the areas where these groups operate in close vicinity of their rivals.

The impact of the new missionary thrust on African culture and national identity is alarming. Whereas the missionaries themselves are confident with regard to the values they come to propagate, the prospective African converts are neither deeply defensive of their own cultural roots, nor sure of their national aspirations. Owing to the influence of the electronic and print media all over the world, the new organizations have become facilitators for the erosion of traditional values in both rural and urban areas.

The challenge posed by these movements is a complex one, with several facets. First, they themselves need to be self-critical, to examine closely whose interests they are serving.

Second, the older missionary-related Churches and institutions, which have a much longer contact with African peoples, also need to continually re-evaluate their work and find new ways of relating both with Africans and with the rival organizations. The Ecumenical Movement still holds great promise, if the campaigns against it can be effectively weathered. Third, Africans need to be educated in various ways to understand the mission-mentality prevalent in Europe and North America. Both African Christians and prospective African converts ought to be equipped with knowledge to enable them to respond firmly in the face of the missionary invasion.

Lastly, national governments need policies to regulate foreign missions just as in the European and North-American countries. Why is it easier for foreign "missionaries" to come to Africa than for African missionaries to go to Europe and North America? It is not just because of lack of funds — there are other more important factors, including that of immigration control.

Conclusion

A mission-mentality and crusading spirit continue to linger in Europe and North America, in spite of the decline of Christianity there. This mentality has largely shifted from Christianity to civil religion. Many people in the North Atlantic countries think, analogically, that the African population is like a clean slate upon which the invading cultures and ideologies can write anything they choose. Another analogy is that of a jar with a narrow neck, which competing cultures and ideologies are trying to fill.

More than twenty years ago, S.C. Neill wrote that five forces were contending for the African soul. That was at the time when many African countries were just about to achieve national sovereignty, or had just achieved it. Neill's observation was typical of the apprehension we have discussed earlier.[26] The five forces, according to Neill, were:

(i)   The old African tradition
(ii)   Sheer materialism
(iii) Communism
(iv)   Islam
(v)   Christianity

He noted that it was not yet clear in whose hands the future of Africa South of the Sahara was to lie. As the twentieth century draws to a close, how would we respond to Neill's portrayal of the African situation?

A similar crusading approach has been presented for the world by Leslie Lyall who compares Christianity and Communism, and complains that by 1972 the communist movement had captured one third of the world in half a century, whereas Christianity was still a minority movement after nearly twenty centuries.[27] The implication is that Christianity should embark on a crusade to reclaim the world "for Christ". How can we respond to this view of Christianity.

First, it is necessary to clarify concepts and avoid confusion. Second, our analysis should, as closely as possible, correspond with the facts. The view that Africans have empty heads and uncommitted souls is erroneous. An African, as a human being, can choose what to believe and what not to. It is true that exposure will increase his options, but he may choose none of those options. He may also, creatively, blend the ideas and construct his own ideology. Unfortunately, when the options are presented, as Neill and Lyall have done, Christianity becomes an ideology rather than a message of hope. It is likely that presented in this way, Africans will not prefer Christianity to any other ideology, because all of them are foreign packages offered like bait by fishermen with their own objectives.

Christianity, understood as Gospel, Good News, is not an ideology. In other words, it can enrich all cultures, all ideologies, all social structures. At the same time, it can purify all, as salt, light and fire. Africans, therefore, do not have to choose between being Christian and being African. They can be both Christian and African at the same time. In any case, both Neill and Lyall, and those others who hold this crusading spirit, are true to their own cultures, to their own national ideologies and to Christianity. Why should Africans not do the same?

The facts and observations made above are intended to help the reader understand and appreciate the social context of Christianity in Africa. Hopefully, their application to any particular African country will yield interesting discoveries and elicit, for the reader, new ways of coping with the challenges that confront Africa today and in future.

1.   Fisher, H.A.L. *A History of Europe, Vol. I, From Earliest Times to 1713*, London: Collins, 1935, esp. Chapters I – XII; *Pears Encyclopaedia*, Chronicle of Events.

2. At the peak of their civilization, the Romans were not interested in research, geographical or otherwise. They were more interested in oratory and rhetoric. See Jerome Carcopino, *Daily-Life in Ancient Rome,* Trans E.O. Lorimer, Yale University Press, 1940. Citation from the Bantam Edition, 1971, pp. 128–129.

3. *Fisher, op. cit.,* pp. 427–31.

4. Chancellor Williams, *The Destruction of Black Civilization,* Chicago: Third World Press, 1970.

5. Carcopino, J. *op. cit.,* p. 272.

6. Several African historians have reconstructed the history of African peoples from oral and archaeological sources, and the link between North Africa and the tropical zone appears historically confirmed. Among the East African historians with research in this aspect are B.A. Ogot, G.S. Were, W. Ochieng and H.S.K. Mwaniki.

7. Neill, S.C. *A History of Christian Missions,* Penguin Books, 1964, pp. 37–38.

8. Neill, S.C. *ibid.*

9. On the notion of *Transportation* in Christian Theology see C.S. Song, *The Compassionate God,* New York: Orbis Books, 1982 pp. 1-17.

10. Sipo Mzimela, *Apartheid: South African Nazism,* Nairobi: Evangel Publishing House, 1983.

11. Neill, S.C. *op. cit.,* pp. 426 ff.

12. Tanzania and Namibia, for example.

13. Russell, B. *A History of Western Philosophy,* London: Allen and Unwin, 1946, 2nd Edition, 1961, pp. 196–205, 444–54; Herbert J. Muller, *The Uses of the Past,* New York: Oxford University Press, 1957, pp. 114–120.

14. Muller, J. *op. cit.,* p. 120.

15. On this point, see James H. Cone, *A Black Theology of Liberation,* Philadelphia/New York. J.B. Lippincott, 1970, pp. 66–74; Eric Williams, *Capitalism and Slavery,* London: Andre Deutsch, 1964; Garth Lean, *God's Politician: William Wilberforce's Struggle,* London: Darton, Longman and Todd, 1980.

16. Paul Johnson, *Caution: God at Work,* New York: Orbis Books, 1976, pp. 27–40.

17. Documentation on Theologies of Liberation is now abundant, though there was hardly any twenty years ago. The Maryknoll Publishing Units called Orbis Books, based in New York, has contributed greatly in recording this theological development.

18. Cone, J. H. *op. cit.,* p. 72.

19. Neill, S.C. *op. cit.,* Chapters 10 and 12.

20. Oliver, Roland *The Missionary Factor in East Africa,* London: Longman, 1952, 2nd Edition 1970, Chapters IV and V; Kenneth J. King, *Pan-Africanism and Education,* Oxford University Press, 1971.

21. This approach to missiology was adopted in *History's Lessons for Tomorrows Mission,* Geneva: WSCF, C. 1960. In that book, several well-known scholars contributed interesting critical essays, including Hendrick Kraemer.

22. Barrett, D.B. *Schism and Renewal in Africa,* London: Oxford University Press, 1968.

23. This linkage continues because of continuing financial support. On the debate about this point, see Elliott Kendall, *The End of an Era: African and the Missionary,* London: SPCK, 1978.

24. The Term "African Independent Churches" has been commonly used, but it is offending to the missionary-linked Churches. "African Charismatic Churches" has been proposed by Mercy A. Oduyoye, and seems more suitable than any others as yet invented. See Mercy A. Oduyoye, "East and West from an African Perspective", in Thomas Wieser, ed. *Whither Ecumenism,* Geneva: WCC, 1986, p. 91.

25. Ample documentation is growing on this subject. For an introduction,

see S.C. Neill, *op. cit.*, pp. 457-60; W. Hollenweger, *Pentecost Between Black and White, Belfast: Christian Journals Ltd., 1974; J.S. Mbiti, Bible and Theology in African Christianity,* Nairobi: Oxford University Press, 1986, pp. 208-41.

26.   Neill, S.C. *op. cit.,* pp. 494–502.

27.   Lyall, Leslie. *A World to Win,* London: IVF, 1972, p. 5.

Chapter Eight

CHRISTIAN BAPTISM
AND THE NAMING OF PERSONS

(A Theological Reflection in the Context of Contemporary Africa)

Introduction

To most ordinary Christians in contemporary Africa, baptism is a Christian ritual in which converts to the Christian faith acquire new names. In most Churches of all confessional families, baptism in Africa is associated with the giving of foreign names to those who are being baptized. This aspect of the ritual of baptism has been so emphasized in Africa that the sacramental significance of baptism has become obscured in the theological understanding of most African Christians including many clergymen and Church leaders.[1]

In modern Africa, it tends to be assumed that a Christian should have at least two names, one which is foreign and one which is 'native'. The practice of giving foreign names to African converts to the Christian faith was introduced by missionaries as an outward reminder to the convert that becoming a Christian implied beginning a new way of life. The first generation of converts tended to be given the names of biblical characters like Abraham, Moses, Joshua, John, Andrew, Simon, Paul, Mark, Luke and so on. Some converts were given the names of early Church Fathers, like Augustine, Athanasius, Clement, and so on. This was especially the case in the Catholic Church. The intention was that these names should remind the converts they should follow the example of those characters after whom they were named.

Later on, however, the names given at the baptism ceased to follow this criterion. Any European name was accepted as suitable for 'Christening' an African convert. As a result, European names which in Europe would normally be surnames have become 'Christian names' in modern Africa. Many Christians in Africa take for granted the notion of 'Christian names'. But what is a 'Christian name?' Is there any scriptural or theological basis for giving new names at baptism?

In Western Churches today the naming of persons does not seem to be associated with the sacramental ritual of baptism. Is there any convincing theological reason why in Africa this practice of giving 'Christian names' should be maintained?

The Faith and Order Commission of the World Council of Churches is in the process of developing a consensus among the member Churches of the WCC, under the theme 'One Baptism, One Eucharist and a Mutually Recognized Ministry'. It seems that until now, ecumenical discussions on baptism have not considered seriously the implications of associating the sacrament of baptism with the cultural practice of naming persons. Perhaps one of the reasons for this omission is that among the older Churches in Europe and North America, this has not been considered a theological problem. In Africa, and perhaps in Asia, however, this is a problem which should be seriously examined. In the final agreed statement on baptism, it will be worthwhile to include a comment on this practice of associating baptism with the naming of persons.[2]

Scriptural Arguments for Associating Baptism with the Naming of Converts

Whenever someone asks for the scriptural basis on which new (usually foreign) names are given to converts and infants at baptism, he is given the example of Abraham, Simon Peter and Paul of Tarsus. It is explained that each of these individuals acquired new names at critical periods in their religious development. Therefore, the argument goes on, it is scripturally justifiable for Christian converts and infants to be given new names at baptism.

However, none of these characters acquired new names at baptism. In any case, the change of Abram's name to Abraham is inappropriate for this argument, because the ritual of baptism had not acquired the religious significance which was accorded to it by John the Baptist, by Jesus and by the Christians of the first century A.D. Abram's change of name to Abraham

(Genesis 17:1–8) was in a very different context.

As for Simon, the brother of Andrew, he was named Peter by Jesus not at his baptism, but at his confession, that Jesus was Christ. Without entering into lengthy exegesis of the passage (Matt. 16:13–20; Mk. 8:27–20; Lk. 9:18–22), it seems that Jesus was playing on words in appreciation of Simon's insight regarding the messianic significance of Jesus. Simon, Andrew, John and James had probably undergone the baptism of John before they became the disciples of Jesus. The gospels do not say that they underwent another baptism (with water) after becoming followers of Jesus. Nor did they acquire new names.

The third case often cited in support of this practice is that of Saul of Tarsus. It is clear, however, that Paul was not a baptismal name for Saul of Tarsus, but probably the Hellenic version of the same Jewish name (Acts 13:9). He was not called Paul immediately after his conversion on the way to Damascus —he continued to be known as Saul, and apparently both names (Saul and Paul) continued to be used interchangeably.

Among the first generation of Christians, baptism continued to be an important ritual (e.g., Acts 3:30; 8:12–13; 10:34–48, etc.). However, no baptism reported in the Acts of the Apostles was accompanied by the giving of new names to converts.

It is interesting to note that the custom whereby colonized peoples adopted the names of their masters is much older than Christianity. Moses was mistaken for an Egyptian by the daughters of the priest of Median (Exodus 2:16–22), perhaps because of his name, his language and other cultural characteristics which he had acquired in his upbringing as an Egyptian prince. During the Babylonian exile, many Jews must have acquired Babylonian names. Likewise, when the Greeks conquered Palestine and imposed their culture on that country, many Jews must have adopted Hellenistic names. The Greek cultural influence was still strong when Christianity began to spread, and it was in the Graeco-Roman setting that Saul was referred to as Paul, and Simon was called Peter. Under the influence of Roman culture many acquired Roman names as well as other aspects of Roman culture.

When Europeans conquered Africa, the same process of acculturation took place. Africans adopted various aspects of the culture of their masters, including foreign names. Since Christianity was the religion of their masters, it seemed to many Africans that accepting it was an outward expression of becoming 'civilized'. They learned this from the missionaries, who believed that evangelization included the spreading of western 'civilization' and the condemnation of African culture. The insights expressed in the Council of

Jerusalem (Acts 15, Gal. 2,3) seem to have escaped the notice of the missionaries despite their literal rendering of the New Testament writings.

The Council of Jerusalem had resolved that cultural identity was important, but that it was of secondary significance as far as conversion to the Christian faith was concerned. Jews and non-Jews could retain their culture and become Christians. No culture was free from the judgement of the gospel. The Modern Missionary Enterprise, in contrast, seems to have created the impression that Western culture was the criterion on which all other cultures must be judged. In maintaining this impression, they were like the Judaizers who were condemned for their cultural arrogance in the Council of Jerusalem.

Owing to the close association of Western Christianity with Western culture during the modern missionary enterprise, baptism in Africa became the ritual through which Africans were admitted into Christianity, thereby becoming partakers of Western civilization. It became like 'circumcision' for Gentiles in their proselytization into Judaism.

John the Baptist and His Baptism

The Gospels present John the Baptist as the forerunner of Jesus. In his ministry, John emphasized that people should repent of their sins so that God might forgive them. Those who repented would be baptized — ritually cleansed in the waters of the river Jordan. For the followers of John, this ritual cleansing in the river Jordan had great symbolic significance. The clean, cool waters of the Jordan sprang from the high mountains of Lebanon, and flowed into the salty, Dead Sea. Those who repented would be totally immersed in this river and, symbolically, their sins should be washed by these clean waters, to be deposited in the Dead Sea. They would abandon their old life and begin to live anew. As a public ritual, this ceremony must have had a profound impact on the lives of John's followers. But the ritual did not involve the acquisition of a new name, foreign or 'native'. Nevertheless, it was so significant that, when Jesus began his public ministry, some people wondered whether he had anything new to add to the teaching of John, which had seemed complete in itself. (Mk. 18–22).

Jesus accepted the public ministry of John but he transcended it. He was baptized by John but John did not give him a new name. In his instruction to Nicodemus, Jesus talked of New Birth, of being 'born of water and the Spirit' (John 3:1–15). The Gospel according to St. John reports that although John the Baptist was the forerunner of Jesus, both were baptizing simultaneously towards the end of John's ministry (John 3:22–36). The emphasis in the teaching of Jesus was on the coming of the 'Kingdom of God'. John the Baptist believed that the ministry of Jesus had transcended his own.

On the basis of the scriptural references where baptism is reported, whether as practised by John, Jesus or the Apostles, it can be concluded that this ritual did not involve the giving or acquisition of new names. There seems to be common agreement that the ritual involved a public ceremony in which those who had repented would undergo a symbolic cleansing, marking the end of the old life and the beginning of a new one characterized by continual repentance. Since baptism under John and Jesus was based on a person's own confession of sins, infant baptism does not seem to have been practised either by John or by Jesus. Apparently, the baptism of households was a later development in the missionary activity of the apostles. This is implied in Acts 11:13–14. Later, in Acts 16, it is reported that Lydia and her household were baptized (Acts 16:15) and also the Jailer 'with all his family' (Acts 16:25–34). In none of these cases did it involve the giving of new names. It seems, therefore, that the association of baptism with the giving of new names to converts has more to do with acculturation (imposed or voluntary) than with Christian sacramental theology.

The Sacramental Significance of Christian Baptism

Although baptism as a religious practice was carried over from the ministry of John the Baptist, in Christianity it became one of the most important customs in ecclesial life. It became the ritual through which new converts were publicly admitted into the Christian community of faith — into the Church. Spiritually, baptism became the ritual in which the convert declared his acceptance of God's free offer of forgiveness. Most Christian Churches regard baptism as a *sacrament*. According to the Anglican Catechism, a sacrament is 'an outward and visible sign of an inward and spiritual grace given unto us, ordained by Christ himself, as a means whereby we receive the same (spiritual grace) and a pledge to assure us thereof'. *(The Book of Common Prayer,* 1969 edition, Oxford University Press, p. 356.)

As regards the sacramental significance of baptism, the Anglican Catechism gives the following instruction:[3]

QUESTION — How many parts are there in a Sacrament?

ANSWER   — Two; the outward visible sign, and the inward spiritual grace.

QUESTION — What is the outward visible sign or form in Baptism?

ANSWER   — Water; wherein the person is baptized *In the Name of the Father, and of the Son, and of the Holy Ghost.*

QUESTION — What is the inward and spiritual grace?

ANSWER   — A death unto sin, and a new birth unto righteousness: for being by nature born in sin, and the children of wrath, we are hereby made the children of grace.

QUESTION — What is required of persons to be baptized?

ANSWER   — Repentance, whereby they forsake sin; and Faith, whereby they steadfastly believe the promises of God made to them in that Sacrament.

QUESTION — Why then are infants baptized, when by reason of their tender age they cannot perform them?

ANSWER   — Because they promise them both (Repentance and Faith) by their Sureties, which promise, when they come to age, themselves are bound to perform.

The Anglican Catechism is a manual for instructing those converts who are being prepared for confirmation. The Catechism assumes that the catechumen are already baptized. The opening questions and answers of that Catechism assume that the catechumen are given 'Christian names' by their godparents at baptism:[4]

QUESTION — What is your name?

ANSWER   — N or M.

QUESTION — Who gave you this name?

ANSWER   — My Godfathers and Godmothers in my Baptism; wherein I was made a member of Christ, the child of God, and an inheritor of the Kingdom of heaven.

It has already been noted that in the New Testament there seems to be no scriptural basis for associating baptism with the naming of persons. In the Anglican Catechism just cited, the explanation of the sacramental significance of baptism does not include a discussion of the relevance of giving names at baptism although this practice is assumed. It is not clear when, in Church history, Christians began associating baptism with the naming and renaming of converts. Though the *Book of Common Prayer* does not state the source of this tradition, the practice has become an integral part of Anglican catechetical instruction. The practice of giving the 'Christian names' needs serious theological reconsideration.

In citing sections of the Anglican Catechism, the author's aim has not been to offer a theological critique of the Anglican understanding of baptism, but to illustrate how Christian baptism is viewed today in the Anglican Communion. It is worthwhile to add that, although the giving of foreign names at baptism is a common practice in the Anglican Church in contemporary Africa, there are some clergymen who do not insist on it. However, this is more the exception than the rule.

One important theological question needs to be seriously discussed: Is the giving of names at baptism of any significance for the converts? In the context of contemporary Africa, it seems that this practice does not have the religious significance which the early missionaries may have intended. Rather, the renaming of children and adults in the sacrament of baptism seems to have obscured the theological significance of that sacrament. This is because, as pointed out at the beginning, most African Christians have tended to regard baptism mainly as the giving or acquisition of foreign names rather than as a sacrament. Viewed in this way, baptism is more culturally, than theologically, significant. The acquisition of a foreign name in addition to the 'native' ones seems to imply the acceptance of Western culture (acculturation) by the convert as an adult, or by the godparents and natural parents who choose the name for the child. Perhaps an emphatic dissociation of the cultural practice of naming from the sacramental practice of baptism would contribute greatly towards restoring baptism to its rightful place in Christian ecclesial life.

When an African Christian chooses to use his African first name rather than his foreign one, he may expect questions such as the following from fellow Christians: 'Are you a Christian? If you are a Christian, are you baptized? If you are baptized, what is your Christian name? If you have such a name, why do you prefer not to use it? Are you ashamed of being a Christian?' Such questions indicate a serious theological misunderstanding of the sacramental significance of Christian baptism. If the early Christians did not need the appendage of foreign names to be added in their baptism, why should African Christians today be burdened with such appendages?

Christian Baptism as a Renaming Ritual in Contemporary Africa

In the African cultural tradition, naming is an important aspect of the life of an individual in the context of his family and community. The name which a child is given at birth defines his identity not merely as a label selected at random, but as a description of his personality in relation to his family, his community and his environment. As in the Old Testament, where Hebrew names were given to children as summary descriptions of their personality, in Africa a child is named after a relative, according to the season of his birth, and so on. Among many African peoples, an individual may be given an additional name during his initiation into adulthood, and this is the name by which his age-mates will know him. Such a 'peer name' is not open for common use by other members of the community. The name so acquired is a further descriptive identification of an individual. It is given to depict a significant trait in the young person's character.

Thus naming is still so important among Africans that some students frequently insist on changing their names when they enter institutions of higher learning so that they may be known by names which are in accordance with their own cultural understanding of themselves. Sometimes such students drop the 'Christian names' which may have been given at their infant baptism. Some foreign observers are puzzled by this apparently strange behaviour and may regard it as an unnecessary reaction against what the students consider to be an aspect of Western cultural domination in Africa. Although it is true that many 'schooled' Africans are reacting against Western cultural domination, it is also true that this insistence on changing names is indicative of the desire, based on the African cultural heritage, to bear names which actually *describe* one's identity, rather than being merely labels picked at random, like numbers in a register. Let these remarks on changing names suffice for the moment, for it is not possible to exhaust this topic here.

The first name *(prenom)* in Western culture is normally the one used among equals and among people who have become acquainted with each other. In the African cultural heritage, this is not the case. Since African Christians normally have more than one first name — including the foreign 'Christian name'—, the application of this Western custom becomes rather inappropriate. Whereas in the Western cultural tradition the use of the first name is an expression of familiarity, in Africa the use of the 'Christian name' is an indication of 'Christianization', 'civilization', 'schooling' and so on. The 'Christian names' are normally given after the 'real' names of a person have been given and popularized. In Kenya, for instance, where the registration of births is being widely implemented, an infant may be issued with a birth certificate before he is baptized. If the baptism of such an infant is understood as a ritual in which he is renamed, the child may later get into legal difficulties, for he will have to swear an affidavit before a Commissioner of Oaths in order to change his name and include the baptismal appendage. Otherwise the godparents have to confirm the registered names instead of adding new ones. As for adult baptism, the same problem remains. When an adult chooses to become a Christian and undergoes baptism, to give him a new name will involve his swearing an affidavit for changing his name so as to include the one given to him at baptism.

Many people in Africa are confused by the term 'surname', because, in the African cultural heritage, a person is known by all his names, which describe his total identity.

It may be concluded, then, that in discussing the Christian theological meaning of baptism in the context of contemporary Africa, the common practice of associating the sacrament of baptism with the cultural practice of naming persons (whether infants or adults) needs to be seriously reconsidered. As suggested earlier on, it will be worthwhile for the WCC Commission on Faith and Order to comment clearly on this practice in the final version of the proposed Agreed Ecumenical Statement on Baptism. Such a comment will help in reducing the theological misunderstanding which looms among many African Christians, that Christian baptism means merely the acquisition of a new (foreign) name.

NOTES

1. The over-emphasis of baptism as a name-giving ritual rather than an ecclesiastical sacrament may be one of the reasons for very little African response to the Ecumenical Consensus on *Baptism Eucharist and Ministry,* Faith and Order Commission, Geneva: World Council of Churches, 1982. See also, William Lazareth, *Growing Together in Baptism Eucharist and Ministry:* A study Guide, Faith and Order Commission, Geneva: WCC, 1982.

2. This comment was inserted at the request of the few Africans who were present at the Faith and Order Conference in Lima, Peru, in January 1982. This author was present. It was clear that many of the commissioners did not fully understand why the issue was raised at all. Thus the comment on this practice did not completely dissociate baptism with naming — it only allowed for tolerance towards those who did not view baptism as a naming ritual.

3. *This Book of Common Prayer,* op.cit., p. 356.

4. *Ibid.,* p. 350.

Chapter Nine

THE PRIMARY BUSINESS OF THE CHURCH

Being in Mission

The business of the Church in society and in the world is *to be in mission*. Yet, it is not enough to say that the business, or the *task* of the church in the world is to be in mission because this has been said again and again. We can say that the twelve disciples of Jesus, whose example we follow, have been called in order to inaugurate a community to proclaim the Good News which Jesus has brought into the world. But that too has all been said before. What, therefore, I have tried to do in this book is to add more content to that statement, that the business of the church in the world is to be in mission. This has been done by looking at the various implications of so being.

Evangelization and Theology

Is it possible to be evangelical without having a theology? It is worthwhile to state what we mean by theology.[1] *Theology* is one of those terms coined from two Greek words, *Theos* and *Logos*. It means organized knowledge, that is, the *Logos* about *Theos,* about God. It is an organized, critical, systematic knowledge about God. So it is possible to go and evangelize without that critical analysis, without that systematic organization. But theology is the attempt to put that which is being done and that which has been done in an orderly fashion so that if someone asks a question, it is possible to show that there is a system; there is an order in what is being done.

Ideally evangelization ought not to be done without theology; but in practice, it has happened and it is happening today. There are people who think that theology spoils the mission of the Church and are very suspicious of those who have been trained in theology or who might want to do theology. There is much reluctance on the part of such people to use critical and analytical tools to examine what ought to be happening in mission.[2] So, this is not a theoretical question.

Ideally, there ought not to be any separation between the work of evangelizing and the work of theologizing. But in practice, in the past and in the present and possibly in the future, that separation is there. The question that was asked by Prof. J.S. Mbiti in the 1970s, and still remains a pertinent question, is how is it possible that the Church can continue to grow numerically in Africa, by leaps and bounds, with very many people becoming Christians everyday, and yet lack a theological justification for that African expression of Christianity.[3] This also is not a theoretical question; it is a real problem.

Our challenge is that, instead of running away from those serious questions that affect the process of evangelization, we should confront them. When one does not have answers to particular questions, it is not ethical to prevent other people from asking those questions or even to shy away from them. The challenge is to try to seek ways of reconciling the apparent contradictions.

Interpreting the Scriptures

One should not run away from the fact that there are some difficulties in handling scriptural text. In the New Testament, for instance, one of the problematic passages is the first chapter of the gospel according to St. John. To say that "in the beginning was the Word and the Word was with God and the Word was God" does not make sense in the English language. One would have to go and find out what it is supposed to mean, because at its face value, it does not make sense at all. When you go to find out what it was supposed to mean, the WORD which is written in capitals, does not mean "Word" in Greek.[4] It means something else. So the challenge we ought to accept is not to run away or to pretend to understand when we do not. Rather, it is the challenge to go and find out more. When one is asked a problematic question by someone whom one goes to evangelize or convince, the solution is not to muffle the person who is asking or tell him that it is a stupid question, or to ask him to go and pray to the Lord. It is better to say that you do not have a solution at the particular time and that you promise to find out; then, you go and find out. If you cannot get a satisfactory answer, look for somebody who knows it, so that you may be helped to solve that question.

The Importance of Theological Education

The ability to resolve such contradictions depends on the quality of theological education.[5] The problem of theological education affects evangelization in the whole continent of Africa, particularly within the older Protestant denominations. The problem of theological education in the Catholic church is rather different. The difference is aptly pointed out by Roland Oliver in this quotation: "The quality of theological education within the Catholic church is very much higher than what it is in the established denominations of the Protestant group".[6] The reason is that the Catholic Church, organized universally, has certain standards that have been established and that have to be met by all people who work within the Church at certain levels of hierarchy. The Catholic Higher Institute of Eastern Africa, for example, is a very high-powered institution which is expected to operate at the same standard of training as the institutions that the Catholic Church has established in Rome. Protestant Churches have as yet no such equivalents in Africa.[7]

Now, when one compares what the Protestant Churches have been able to achieve in theological education with the Catholic effort, the qualities might not probably be even half of what the Catholic Church has accomplished. Why is this?

It is difficult to find one answer to the problem because it has a long and complex history. It has to do with the history of Protestant missions in Africa. That is part of the reason. It also has to do in part with the Protestant formation during the colonial period as well as with the dynamics of foreign aid. And it also has to do with the understanding that most Protestant denominations had of how theological education ought to be conducted, particularly during the colonial period. For instance, John Mbiti has observed that many of the people who evangelized Africa, who established Christianity here, were themselves not theologians.[8] And to a large extent this continues to happen.[9] It also happens, as Roland Oliver has observed, that many of the activities that were associated with Christian missions were really not evangelization in the way that we have talked about it in this book.[10]

The activities of the majority of the Protestant missionaries had to do more with acculturation (with getting the people in the colonies to accept the cultural norms of the country from which the missionaries came) than with getting them to understand the scriptures. Now why has this lingered on for so long?

Well, to change social structures is not an easy thing and it cannot be done overnight. There is a need for a conscious effort to plan in the long term in order to correct the mistakes done in the past. Unless there is careful planning, change for the better is not just going to happen by chance. In order to understand why this happened with regard to Protestant theological education, we should not look for one answer. We have to see the whole complex, the whole scenario within which these shortcomings have happened. And then, to do something about the shortcomings, we shall have to plan, and plan many years ahead.

Practices and Ideas

It may appear as if the picture I portray of Christianity is very idealistic. Yes, it is idealistic because that is what it is meant to be. Perhaps one of the problems we have in Africa, generally and collectively, is that we lack utopias. At the time when Europe was emerging from its dark ages, much of the literature that enabled it to move from its darkness was utopian literature, beginning from Erasmus to Thomas More to John Locke to Thomas Hobbes, to Jean Jacques Rousseau. Those thinkers were trying to find out what kind of society, a good society, ought to be. Without such utopias, there is no way a society can transform itself. We need to distinguish here between what *we want* and what *we ought to want*. The two are not the same.

Christianity does give us some indication of the direction we ought to be following, and the goals we ought to attain. Even when we know that we are not perfect, we should be able to check what we do against what we know we ought to be doing. In one of the confessions in Christian liturgy, there is a prayer in which we say that we have not done what we ought to have done; and we have done what we ought not to have done. This ought to be a constant reminder for us, irrespective of what role and what status we hold in society or in Church.

To suggest that Christianity is idealistic is not to say something negative — it is to say something positive about it. Christianity gives us the aspiration to do better, in spite of our limitations.

The difference between us and Jesus is that in Jesus, there is total integration between the "ought" and the "is". There is so much integration that the ideal and the actual are identical in Jesus. For many of us, the difference between the ideal and the actual is so great that we give up trying to integrate our efforts with our ideals. What we ought to be trying to do is always to ensure that the ideal and the actual are as close as possible, even though it is not easy to reduce the gap to nil.

African Christian Theology

The African Christian ought to affirm both his faith and his culture in the same way that the European individual is proud to affirm that he is a Christian and a European at the same time.[11] Why should Africans be exceptions to this rule? The first step is to distinguish and separate between the Christian scriptures and other Christian literatures because the two categories are different. It is true that the finalization of the Canon was done within the cultural and philosophical framework of Europe. It is also true that if the settlement of the Canon (that is, the books that have been accepted as constituting the New Testament) were done in another culture, probably other books would have been included which are not now included. It is the cultural and philosophical factor that distinguishes the Septuagint from the earlier Canon. Be that as it may, it still happens to be true that even with the Canon which the Churches of the World have ecumenically accepted as the minimum sufficient for scriptural authority, there are many other things that have been adopted from European culture in the name of Christianity, which have nothing to do with the scriptures. As a matter of fact, many practices associated with Christianity as we know it today have no direct reference in the basic scriptures. Many norms that have been accepted as Christian norms have no direct reference in the scriptures; they have only an indirect reference without a definite sanction.

When separation has been done between scriptural authority and ecclesiastical tradition, it is then possible for the African to ask himself what difference it makes for him to have become a Christian.[12] When he reads the scriptures himself, or when the scripture is read to the African who cannot read, the question is: What does he hear, what does he read? It is the experience of many Africans that when they read the scriptures themselves, and when they hear the interpretation by somebody else from another culture, they do not derive the same meaning. What the African hears when he reads for himself or when the scriptures are read to him is what ought to prevail. But what he is *being told* that the scriptures are saying, that he ought to put aside. Now to be able to do that, one needs much confidence, much conviction, much courage and much diplomacy. One ought to thank the person who evangelizes one. "Thank you very much for bringing the gospel to me, I value it very much. But what you are telling me that the scriptures are saying is not what I *see*. You are still my brother in Christ, you are still my sister in Christ. But please let the gospel speak to me directly." An African Christian needs courage to say this to the missionary who introduces Christianity to him. One has to be as polite as possible in order to get that message across. Those who bring the scriptures to us have also to be humble enough to accept that finally it is God who wins souls. It is not we who win souls for anybody. We are not capable of doing that. We can only become agents to enable God to win our souls; but we cannot win souls ourselves.

Now to articulate that message and state it as humbly and as diplomatically and clearly as possible, without hurting the feelings of those who have introduced the scriptures, is not very easy. Nevertheless, those fundamental issues of Christian theology which were debated during the early councils from Nicea to Trent need to be rediscussed by African Christian theologians. The process of discussion has started, but we are hardly half-way through. Thoses questions will have to be asked again: What does God mean for an African Christian? God meant that which has been formulated in the Nicene creed, in the Apostles creed, at that time, among those people. Are those formulations the same formulations that we want to uphold, or do we need to look at them again?

Such discussion will have to be in the context of the African world-view and of the basic values in African understanding. With regard to cultural practices, a distinction should be made between three things which are very often confused; social practices, social structures and basic values.

Values, Structures and Practices

Within any given society, even without outside influence, these things change in time. The basic values and world-views are the last to change. For example, many schooled Africans still presuppose the traditional world-view, including the notion of duration, in spite of having been taught to adopt the Western (scientific) world-view. According to traditional African thought, the day begins at dawn and ends at dusk; whereas the "modern" world-view teaches that the day begins and ends at midnight. In ordinary conversation, schooled Africans shift from the one world-view to the other, depending on the language they use. We already have two different world-views there and we are every now and then, almost unconsciously, shifting in our own culture from the African way of measuring time to the European.

If then we are convinced that certain basic values in the African tradition are worthwhile, what ought to happen is that with the change of society as a result of pressures historical, social, political, economic, religious and so on, some social structures have to be modified. But social structures are rather difficult to modify, less difficult, perhaps, than basic values but certainly more so than individual practices.

Social structures may have to be modified from generation to generation in order to maintain basic values. Practices are easiest to change in society. They have to be modified at the level of the individual, the level of the family, only in order to keep the basic values intact. Now if someone says that he is doing certain things in order to preserve African culture, and he is talking only at the level of practices and not of the basic values, then he is not speaking the whole truth.

So when we look at a particular practice, African practice, and we want to defend it in the name of African culture, we should not only look at the practice itself or at the social structure within which it is located. We should look at the basic value and world-view which justified it in the first place. And the question to ask is: "That particular practice, when it was done, why was it done? What was intended?" This is because when it was started, it had something very positive about it. What was it intended to achieve? What value was it intended to uphold? The basic value ought not to be compromised. Now, it may mean then that a particular practice that has become offensive in society may have to be modified in order for the basic value to be maintained. This is a necessary procedure irrespective of whether there is a foreign influence or not. Yet even without the influence, this procedure is necessary. The best way to approach this discussion is to separate the basic values from the practices so that we shall be free to modify the practices in order to preserve the traditional values we cherish.

A Lesson From Paul

What ought to be changed and influenced by Christianity is the basic world-view itself. My analysis indicates that there really is not a very serious conflict when it comes to comparing the ideals of Christianity and the basic values of the African heritage. The conflict comes particularly with the practices and with the social structures because these are really derived from another cultural setting. An African needs to have a direct access to Christianity through the African values rather than through some other cultural channel.

In his letters to various Christian communities, Paul uses a theological approach which is instructive for all Christians. After solving a particular problem of the particular community which he addresses, Paul establishes a theological principle applicable in other situations. If he is not sure of such a principle, he makes a distinction between what he thinks and what he knows that God is saying. His teaching about marriage is a case in point (I Cor. 8).

It follows that Paul's general theological principles should be separated and distinguished from the actual practices which he recommends as solutions to particular pastoral problems for the specific Christian communities to whom he writes. The principles, like basic values and world-views, have general relevance and universal applicability; whereas practices have only local relevance in time. Such an interpretation of Pauline theology can help us to appropriate the Christian faith in a variety of cultural and historical situations without distorting the Gospel.

NOTES

1. See chapter six above. Paul Tillich, *Systematic Theology,* Vol. 1, *op. cit.,* Introduction.

2. According to their view, the Bible is sufficient as the source of everything that needs to be communicated in evangelization. Thus their training sessions consist in "Bible Studies" without "theologizing". However, translation and interpretation of the Bible must inevitably presuppose particular hermeneutic principles, which are theologically derived and formulated. Theology is inescapable. The problem is that when we try to avoid it, we end up with undigested theology that may not serve us adequately in times of crisis.

3. See Introduction above. J.S. Mbiti, *New Testament Eschatology in an African Background, op. cit.,* p. 188.

4. Alan Richardson, *Creeds in the Making,* London: SCM Press, 1943.

5. See Chapter Six above.

6. Roland Oliver, *The Missionary Factor in East Africa, op. cit.,* Introduction, (xi).

7. They may not need such equivalents since they aspire for autonomy from their parent denominations abroad. However, it is necessary that the quality of theological education in Africa should be at least comparable to secular and general education in the public institutions. Failure to achieve comparable standards will make it hard for graduates of Bible colleges and seminaries to win credibility. The Commission for Higher Education is charged with the responsibility of standardization in Kenya. This problem had been highlighted in R. Pierce Beaver, ed., *Christianity and African Education,* Grand Rapids, Michigan: Eerdmans, 1966. Also, Kenneth James King, *Pan-Africanism and Education: A Study of Race, Philanthropy and Education in the Southern States of America and East Africa,* London: Oxford University Press, 1971.

8. Alluding to Elliot Kendall, Mbiti notes that the motivation of the Modern Missionary enterprise from Europe to Africa was primarily anthropological rather than theological.

Many of the missionaries came in connection with the abolition of the slave trade and the rehabilitation of freed slaves. David Livingstone's campaign for the missionary enterprise was encapsulated in two words — Commerce and Christianity. There wa no emphasis on rigorous theological training for protestant missionaries coming to Africa. Consequently, protestant theological education in Africa has remained undeveloped, although missionary societies sponsored model primary and secondary schools as well as vocational centres. See J.S. Mbiti, *Bible and Theology in African Christianity, op.cit.,* pp. 189–96; Elliot Kendall, *The End of an Era: Africa and the Missionary,* London: SPCK, 1978.

9. Since 1970 the present author has been occasionally invited to address groups of European and North American missionaries needing orientation at the beginning of their contracts in various parts of tropical Africa. The missionaries come from a wide range of professions, with only a few coming for theological education. What has been striking, however, has been the lack of interest in the theological basis for their missionary involvement. The anthropological, idealogical and economic motivations still predominate over evangelistic and theological ones.

10. Roland Oliver, *The Missionary Factor in East Africa, op.cit.,* Also, J.N.K. Mugambi, *The African Heritage and Contemporary Christianity, op.cit.*

11. This insight is discussed extensively in J.N.K. Mugambi, *African Christian Theology: An East African Perspective,* Nairobi: Heinemann, 1989. See also, J.S. Mbiti, *New Testament Eschatology in an African Background, op.cit.,* pp. 188–91; *Bible and Theology in African Christianity, op.cit.,* pp. 176–227.

12. The separation between scriptural authority and ecclesiastical authority generated the conflict between Martin Luther and the Roman Curia. This separation is what Paul Tillich calls the Protestant Principle. See *Systematic Theology,* Vol. Three, *op.cit.,* Part V. Section 2. The argument in the present chapter is not derived from the Protestant Principle as alluded above. Rather, it is based on the recognition that the Church, both in singular and in plural, derives its mandate from the revelation of God in Jesus of Nazareth, whom Christians affirm, in faith, to be Christ.

13. The view expressed here is at variance with that promoted by people who regard Africa as a spiritual battlefield, where they can win their booty according to their own effort. Africans are capable of responding to God directly, through the Holy Spirit, not via ideological campaigns sugar-coated with evangelism. On this point see Charles P. Conn, *Brother Andrew: Battle for Africa,* London: Marshall, Morgan and Scott, 1977; Ernest W. Lefever, *Amsterdan to Nairobi: The World Council of Churches and the Third World,* cited in Leon Howell, *Acting in Faith, op.cit.,* Leslie Lyall, *A World to Win,* London: Inter-Varsity Press, 1972; Paul Gifford, *The Religious Right in Southern Africa,* Harare: Baobab Books and University of Zimbabwe Press, 1988.

Chapter Ten

MISSION AS THE BE-ALL AND END-ALL OF THE CHURCH

Mission as a Process of Liberation

The task of the church, we have said, is to be in mission. But very often when the word *mission* is used, it is very much with reference to people going to say some words to people who supposedly have not heard them before in the hope that when they do, they will be willing to accept the message and they in turn repeat it to others. So mission is very often associated with the verbal activity in which some people say some things while others listen. But I think it is worthwhile to consider mission in a much more extensive perspective; in a much more complex setting, because when Jesus proclaims the Good News, in fact very little of his activity in that mission is verbal communication.[1]

We know that Jesus is involved in mission when we read the passage that also helps us to know that Jesus was literate. It is the only text that makes us know that Jesus could read and write. That was the text that Jesus read in a small synagogue out in the rural areas and not in Jerusalem. Jesus picked the scroll and read Isaiah chapter 62:1-2 which we find in Luke chapter 4:16-22: "The Spirit of the Lord is upon me, he has annointed me to proclaim good news to the poor, to announce release to the captives; and to announce the year of the Lord." But how does this Jesus go on to proclaim the Good News? We find him not talking about the people getting better when they are ill; we actually find him healing. We find him not going to pray for people who were captives of their own social structures; of their own emotional limitations; we do not find him just praying for them; we find him actually releasing them from whatever is binding them; we find him in activity and what Jesus would refer to as *mission*, as *Good News,* is not what he says; but *what he does.* The action and the words are so integrated that it is impossible to separate the words from the deeds.

Unfortunately, in the history of mission, something happened somewhere and the words and the deeds were separated. This is a mistake that we would do well to correct within our own situation in the future.

Mission as Good News

Mission involves a communication process as we have already seen, and every communication process has got its own mechanisms, its own dynamics, and I shall want us to spend a little time to look at the dynamics or the mechanisms or the interactions of mission. We shall also have occasion to study in greater detail what the message of mission is. For the time being, let me just say that I understand mission to be healing in wholeness. If mission is understood to be the proclamation of Good News and if this is not wholesome healing, then it is not Good News. And I have a suspicion that when we read or hear news and consider that it is good news and are excited about it, it is because we feel some sense of fulfilment. We feel that our expectations have been fulfilled; we feel that some of our friends or relatives have had some fulfilment, and this is why it is considered good news. It is bad news if some frustration is experienced; if some of the things we expected are not what comes, it is bad news.

Unfortunately, in very much of what has been called Christian mission, the proclamation of that which has been presented as Good News has, in fact, not sounded like Good News. It has sounded as terribly bad news. If you go to proclaim a message to somebody, thinking that it is good news and it turns out to be bad news, you know you are terribly embarrassed while the other person gets terribly angry.[2]

Is it possible that we can communicate the Christian message in such a way that indeed it is good news, which is what it is meant to be? For that to happen, the news would have to be proclaimed in such a way that it brings wholeness, healing, and fulfilment. It has to be that way and for that to happen, it is of great importance and necessity that the person who is proclaiming the Good News understands his addressee thoroughly so as to know his expectations, needs and so on. That is the only way in which you can actually be able to proclaim a message such that it is Good News. Jesus was excellent in this because when he was dealing with lawyers, they would talk about law. Whe he was dealing with peasants, they would talk about the problems of peasants out there. When he was talking with fishermen he would talk about fishing.

And he would talk about fishing men instead of fishing fish. But, such is the context in which one is able to communicate. If you understand the expectations, the needs, and the social environment of the other, you will be able to convey the Good News.

The Medium of Mission

The medium of mission is also very important to understand. If we say that mission is a communication process, then we can borrow a few concepts from those who are experts in technical communication. The language is important, the channels that are used for communication are also important and so are the links, because if one of the links is missing, then you cannot have communication.

The social environment in which communication happens is also of great importance as technical experts know. In telecommunication, for example, the capacitors and related gadgets have to be tropicalized if they are in the tropics and they have to be made in a different way if they are in a different environment. If you are in a very cold climate, then the equipment has to be such that it can stand very low temperatures, while in a very hot climate. you have to make it in such a way that it can stand the high temperatures.

The same applies to communicating the Christian mission, but here the receiver of the message is also important. When you want to buy a radio receiver, your choice will depend on how much you want to spend on it; but if you really want to have a good receiver, you must also be interested in the models because some are better than others. You must be interested in the specifications as to whether it has short-wave and/or medium-wave reception; i.e. how far it can go in receiving. You need to be interested in all these details. And so with the Christian mission. If you are involved in a communication process, you need to understand the receiver too. And you need to know the specifications if you expect your message to be effective.

The impact is perhaps the most important of all aspects of the communication process. What do you expect? What do we expect when we involve ourselves in this business of mission, in this business of communication?

We can see that it is possible to assess our impact in quantitative terms. We may, for instance, want to have so many Bibles printed; so many Bibles distributed in such and such a language; we may expect to build so many schools; or within our schools to increase our streams; we may be interested in increasing the number of hospital beds or in the number of clinics; we may be interested in increasing the number of places of worship which are sometimes called churches or we may be interested in increasing the number of converts within our membership. These are quantitative terms; but we could also assess the impact in qualitative terms. And when you come to assess your success in these terms, it is very interesting to observe what happens.

It may turn out that the more quantity you have, the lower the quality achieved. And it is very important that the relationship between the quantity of the impact and its quality be clearly understood. You may, for instance, if you are in one of the projects, be interested in seeing an expansion of your work in quantitative terms. But, it is also equally important to raise the question as to the qualitative change in the behaviour of the people who are expected to receive the message that you intend to communicate.

We said that the fundamental task of the Church is to be in mission and that mission is a communication process. What does this communication process entail? First, of course, we must have a message and this message we presume is coming from God, and it has been received by people with a conviction that they have to proclaim what God has said. We have the sender who sends the message. In order for this sender to be able to send the message, he must have a language. We have coded that language as the first language because most probably it is the language in which the sender himself received the message in the first place. But the moment that you codify your message in the language in which you want to communicate, what happens?

What happens is that the message that you are intending to send out is not in fact the original message that you got from wherever you got it. You have to codify it in such a way that it can actually be sent.

This seems to happen with us even when, for instance, we want to put our information in writing. What we say orally and what we say in writing are two different things. So the message that is received will have to be a different message from the message which the sender had in the first place. What about the medium?

The medium too is very important. The communication process will very much depend on the medium through which it is being conducted as well as our understanding of it. If you are in a medium in which there is a lot of interference, you may have to shout. I am using the word "shout" here analogically because I am aware that in Nairobi when sometimes a mission is understood as shouting, indeed in order to compete with the noise of the buses, and of the matatus and so on, those who are using loudspeakers have to really shout in order to take account of the medium in which their communication process is taking place.

If we do not understand the medium, then our communication process is likely to be affected. But once we understand it and we take account of its qualities, the original message has to be altered. It may not have required shouting to get across; it may not have required repetition, but because of our understanding of the medium, the message becomes affected and has to be changed to take account of the variables of the medium. So we end up with another language, because the language also changes. And using the example I have just given of street preaching in Nairobi, you appreciate that the language has to change because of the medium in which the communication process is taking place. And where people otherwise were speaking normally, they begin to shout at the top of their voices so that even their own manner of speaking becomes affected. Consequently a new language evolves in this process.

By the time the message reaches the receiver, or the recipient, you see that the distance from the original sender and the original message has been completely changed. There has been a complete change in the whole of this process. But in order for effective communication to take place, we have to pay attention to this component as well. If we understand the receiver (that is, if we are talking technically) if we understand our radio receiver, we probably will be able to pick the signals that we want, we will be able to tune in much better than if we do not.

Likewise, if we understand the recipient (talking about social communication) perhaps we will be able to tune in much better than if we do not. Where we have not taken account of the recipient, we are assuming that the whole process of communication is such that the receiver or the recipient is just there to receive. But from the analogy that we are using here, if you have your radio and it is very good and you want to listen to the news if you have not actually taken that radio and do not actually switch on the power; and you do not actually tune finely, you are not going to get any communication. And it is much the same with mission.

The recipient is crucially important, for you will not be effectively communicating, even after having taken care of these things, until you can account for the recipient. But if you have not taken care of the recipient himself, or herself, you may not communicate at all. Yet when you take account of this fact, you get a new message again. The original message had undergone so much transformation, as a result of taking care of these variables, that by the time it actually gets to the recipient, it is a very different message. But hopefully, if the original message that you want to communicate is still there, you can hope that the receiver becomes a sender who also then begins to communicate.

The reader may have participated in the game of communication which is popular with many educators and which illustrates this point. You start with a short sentence. Participants stand in a line and a message is articulated to the first person who is expected to pass it on to the next participant. The experience is usually that by the time the message gets to the other end of the line, it is completely different from what it was originally. This is the challenge of the communication process.

Fortunately, for the Christian mission, there is a corrective. This is because at least you can go back to the scriptures and check as to whether the original message is in fact what has been communicated. How do we relate this to the phenomenon of the rise of the Independent Churches in Africa?

The Independent Church movement in Africa can be explained in terms of what we have analysed here. By the time the message got to the African, it sounded so strange because it seemed that what was being proclaimed and what God was supposed to be saying were not one and the same thing, especially regarding justice, equality, and the question of the distribution of resources and so on. When the African wanted to beg the question, to ask whether in fact what was being said came from God, he would be told it was all there, all there in the Bible.

So the African wanted to learn to read and write in order to be able to go through the process himself. And when he got hold of the Bible, and he read it himself, he said "Ha! What you are saying is not what I find; I am finding something different!" And researches have shown that the rise of the independent churches in Africa is very closely and directly related to the translation of the scriptures in the languages of the people. Where the Bible has not been available in translation there has been a lower level of independency than in those areas where it has been.

So, fortunately, there is that corrective. But even then, throughout this process, we have to be aware that the language and the message undergo changes and correctives as the communication processs persists. Our challenge is to ensure that the message does not become diluted or distorted while it is going through all this process. And this is a very difficult challenge. But there is no other way because if we want to be faithful to the sender, to the original sender, then we have the responsibility of ensuring that the message is not lost through the various components of the communication process.

The Message in Christian Mission

This message is supposed to be good news, "the gospel". We have suggested that if it is good news, it cannot do anything other than wholesome healing. But if we talk about it as wholesome healing, human beings live in community and as members of the community they have to operate within social structures which have been evolved over a long period of time and which have to follow certain principles. So on the one hand, we have the theoretical construction of the social structures and there are many approaches to social organization, and on the other we have the practices which each individual must and is expected to adhere to.

On the theory aspect of it, we may see every society as having five pillars: The pillar of: Economics, which has to do with the distribution of resources within the society; Ethics, which has to do with the value system, particularly with regard to the behaviour between the members of the society — the moral values of the society; Politics, which has to do with the distribution of social influence.

Then there is Aesthetics, which has to do with our understanding of values other than moral values; what we consider to be beautiful; what we consider to be ugly, and so on. But note that when we talk about aesthetics, when we talk about beauty and ugliness, this has really to do with our own evaluation, with the evaluation of our own selves in relation to our social environment and the natural environment and also in relation to our understanding of what our being in the world is all about. And finally a very important pillar within our social structures, what I call here Metaphysics or simply the world-view within which we do all our things and within which we make all our evaluation.

Every society has its metaphysics; every society has its world-view. Later on we shall come to the importance of this world-view, this metaphysics in relation to the process of communication.

Now, if we are talking about wholesome healing, then for communication of the Christian message to be effective it has to be such as to heal in a wholesome way. This social environment has to be such that it can see itself as being healed by the Christian message. If this does not happen, then the Christian message is seen as bad news by that social environment and the people are very upset about it.

When we look at the individual level of this on the practices of the particular individual, what we find is that the Christian message is expected to bring about wholesome healing on the part of the individual himself. And here we get the familiar words about healing — the physical aspects of the human person, his mental, emotional as well as intellectual aspects. When you add up all these components within the social environment, what we get is that at the level of theory and social structures, if we leave out God as the source of the message, we get ideology. Ideology is the summarized formula for the organization of a society's programme.

On the other hand, when we add up all these expectations of the individual, we get the spiritual dimension of the individual expectations. Note that my usage of the term spiritual here is rather general and I am not talking about the Holy Spirit in this particular context. I am suggesting that the whole integration of the human person has to do with the spiritual welfare of the person. All medical practitioners know now that in order for the full health of the person to be restored, it is necessary that all these ingredients be viewed in totality. Thus, the spiritual welfare of the person is just as important as all the other aspects. Emphasis on any one component really does not do justice to the total welfare of the person.

So a person who who can be said to be healthy is one in whom all these components have been taken care of. And there can be no spiritual welfare when any of the components are neglected. The person who has got full spiritual welfare is one who is in control of all the various dimensions of his human life.

Now, it is worthwhile here to look at the relationship between ideology on the one hand and theology on the other. The question is often asked whether theology itself is not an ideology. The answer is this: That indeed there is no theology which has no ideology. And if any one suggests that he is proclaiming a theology without an ideology, he is open to suspicion because the amount of ideology that is concealed in that very claim is so much that it may be the only item that is being communicated!

The unfortunate situation is that for an ideology, the starting point may only be what we ourselves think is good for us. For theology there is always a corrective — the same corrective that you observe in the dynamics of mission. God is there watching, and we can always be able to check what we are doing and the arguments we may be having against the concepts of the Gospel.

So whereas for theology it is possible for us to reason together among ourselves; to reason together with God; to reason together with those who have come before us; to check whether we may have made a mistake and to retrace our steps again; for ideology, irrespective of what ideology we are talking about, there is no way of resolving it except by fighting. If you do not agree to what I am saying, then the only way we can resolve our differences is to determine who is more powerful than the other and if I am more powerful, then my ideology reigns. But when ideology is corrected by theology, there is the chance that people can be able to reason together because the starting point is above what the human beings themselves want.

We cite just one illustration of this, in as far as Paul is concerned. Paul is the first of the Christian theologians to try articulate a theology which was capable of being correlated and contrasted with the Roman and Hebrew ideologies. Paul selects three concepts as guiding principles — Faith, Hope and Love (1 Cor: 13). Faith, Hope and Love — these three abide, but the great, he says, is Love.

Within the ecumenical discussion today, particularly beginning from the early 1970s, from the time of the WCC 5th assembly, three other concepts are used, promoted and popularized. They are intended to remove the discussion from the framework of the Christian scriptures and also to communicate in an increasingly secularized world. These concepts are *participation, sustainability* and *Justice*.[3] My suggestion here is this: Our aspiration for faith, hope and love and our secular quest for participation, sustainability and justice are not really at variance. We could say that in the secular setting, faith is very closely related to sustainability. We cannot grow in our own faith unless there are people in whom there is a community in which we participate and the participation of others in our own faith enhances our own growth as believers.

If we do not have faith in ourselves, we cannot have faith in others. And if we do not have faith in others, neither can we be able to proceed in our own faith. The element of participation is also important. Hope is also important but so is sustainability. The relationship between hope and sustainability is very interesting. In our quest for sustaining our social structures, our economic structures, our political structures and so on, we hope that it is in fact possible to sustain them. And if we have hope, we are assuming that at least what we consider to be important now, what we consider to be valuable, ought in fact to be sustained. So the element of hope and the element of sustainability are very closely interrelated.

Love, which Paul says is the greatest, can also not function where there is no justice. In fact, one must say that the greatest manifestation, the most clear manifestation, of love is justice. Even when we are talking about the relationship between two persons, if one says that one loves another and one does not want to be fair to the person that one says one loves, then of course, we have exploitation. Love presupposes. The close relationship between love and justice is very important. So I am suggesting that perhaps in our discussion of participation, sustainability and justice, we try to read again (1 Cor: 13).

Our talk about the biblical concepts of faith, love and hope, and the secular concepts of sustainability, participation and justice, leads us to raise a question about the relationship between salvation and liberation. Salvation is a term which very often is in the mouths of those who are proclaiming the word of God as Christians. Liberation is the word which is very much found among those who are interested in the secular concerns of participation, sustainability and justice. I wish to suggest that these two words which have come to be separated ought, in fact, not to be in conflict. In the Bible, in both the Old and the New Testaments, there is no conflict between the concern for salvation and the concern for liberation. In fact, there is no separation. We might say that any quest for salvation which does not take socio-political issues seriously is going to be rendered irrelevant and is going to be terribly bad news to the people who are in need of socio-political fulfilment. But the converse is also true. Any programme that seeks to bring about socio-political and economic fulfilment without a corrective that is transcendental is bound to be incomplete and is bound to be misused at one time or other.

NOTES

1. The public ministry of Jesus lasted about three years. His sayings are summarized in just a few sections of the gospels. Many of the things that Jesus did are only mentioned, not described. The text in Luke 4:16–22 (Isaiah 61:1–2) refers not to verbal communication but to a total individuals and communities. A wholistic view of mission ought to promote evangelization as an integrated combination of proclamation, service and community enhancement.

2. There have been cases when missionaries have been expelled from a country because of abusing the sovereignity and cultural integrity of the people they claimed to evangelize. This ought not to happen in genuine Christian evangelization. St. Paul respected and appreciated the culture of the people he went to evangelize. He was willing and ready to debate with them. Yet many Christian missionaries today, especially those from Europe and North America, tend to suffer from a superiority complex which prevents them from interacting effectively with those whom they come to evangelize. Jesus and Paul have offered approaches and attitudes which every missionary ought to emulate. See Roland Allen, *Missionary Methods: St. Pauls or Ours?* London: Lutterwoth, 1968; *History's Lessons for Tomorrows Mission, op.cit.*

3. The themes of participation, sustainability and Justice were widely debated in the Ecumenical Movement between the WCC 5th and 6th Assemblies (Nairobi; 1975 and Vancouver 1983). Arising from those debates new themes emerged, to be debated between the 6th and 7th Assembly (Canberra, Australia, 1991) — Justice, Peace an Integrity of Creation. For a contribution to the debate see J.N.K. Mugambi, *God, Humanity and Nature in Relation to Justice and Peace,* Geneva: World Council of Churches, 1987.

Chapter Eleven

THE CULTURAL CONTEXT OF MISSION

We might say that salvation as an eschatological quest which is always beyond us is one side of the same coin of human fulfilment, the other side being liberation which is the quest for human fulfilment within history; within the socio-political and economic structures of our time.[1] This leads us to look at the social structures in greater detail.

We have talked about the pillars within society as being economics, ethics, politics, aesthetics and metaphysics. Think of those circular huts that we build and remember that in order for the hut to stand, you need poles. Then think of these pillars as the poles for that hut; our own social environment. Think also of the rafters that join the poles in order to complete the hut.

Now, in order for us to be able to construct the hut in such a way that it stands, it is of great importance that the poles that we select are strong, the rafters that we use are straight, that those that go up and those that go around the poles also meet the purpose for which they are intended. The person who stands at the top of the hut during the construction is in a better position to see whether that hut is actually rounded, properly rounded, or not. If you are at any one of the sides, you cannot know whether the hut is properly round or not. Only the top position gives the commanding view. Similarly our analysis is from the centre in order that we can see the completeness of our circle. But our understanding of the social structures in which we are will very much be influenced by the position where we are. If, for instance, we hide ourselves at one corner of religion, what is likely to happen is that we might see the ethics and aesthetics pillars from the perspective of the metaphysics. We might forget about economics and politics. But that will not enable us to understand fully the society in which we are. Nevertheless, it is also possible for somebody else to analyse society from the perspective, of politics and probably take account of economics, while he forgets the ethics and metaphysics.

But one cannot effectively appreciate society in that way. It is greatly important that we are closer to the centre, as close to the centre as possible; that will enable us to understand the operation of society comprehensively.

Now, a successful Christian mission project is one which is as close to the centre of society as possible in order that it can be able to relate to each one of those pillars. I wish to suggest that this process of connecting with the pillars of society is what we call technology. This may sound rather surprising as a definition of technology, but I suggest that this really is what technology is about. Let us explain what we mean by this concept.

Technologies are *logos* about the *techne* — organized knowledge about tools: how to determine the purpose of the tools that we want to design, to manufacture, to distribute, to defuse, to install, to operate, to maintain, to replace and also to improve. All these are components of technology. In order for the human being to make tools, there is one step that is very important, and I think it is this step that distinguishes the human being from the higher primates.

We have been taught that man is distinguished from the higher primates by the fact that he is a tool-maker. Man is the technological animal. The earliest of the tools that archaeologists have found are connected with hunting and gathering. But it has been found that the higher primates too know how to hunt and to gather. Some of them even know how to throw a stone at a fruit so that it falls. And the original tools that human beings used are not things that they made but objects from the environment. It seems to me that technology starts earlier than the use of objects, natural or artificial. Technology begins when man learns to communicate with others. Technology begins with language. Thus the first tool that man made which distinguishes him from the other animals is *language*. That is what we have been talking about from the beginning.

Language as Technology

When we are able to say what we think in such a way that we can remember it tomorrow, and be able to communicate with another person what we think, then indeed we are differentiating ourselves from other animals. Language as a tool is very important and, depending on the way we use it, we shall be either understood or misunderstood.

The question is not whether we should communicate or not, because as human beings we have to communicate. The question is, how do we communicate? How do we use language? In every language, it is possible to say one thing in different ways. Once you have learnt to use the language, it is not necessary that you are told in clear terms what the person wants to say, because there are, in fact, three different ways of saying it: you can say it to indicate that you do not approve; you can say it to indicate that you approve; and you can also hold a neutral position. The most important concepts have a synonym and an antonym and some neutral words which can be used not to indicate which opinion you support. This is normal in language.

Now, language can be analysed at three levels. First, at the level of nurture — the level of upbringing when the child is growing up to be a human being. At this level, all the child knows is to cry, or to smile, or to sleep and so on. But the mother is able to know whether the child is comfortable or not. When it cries, the mother has to rush to find out what has gone wrong. And when the mother comes, takes the child and rocks it, the child feels comfortable. It knows that it is secure because there are no enemies — it is protected. That too is language: the basic language; the very first language that we learn, is the language of nurture.

But there is another level of language analysis — the level of culture.[4] It is really the cultural level of language which is of greatest interest to us here, because, when we talk about communicating the Christian message, we are talking about using the cultural instruments, including words, in order to be able to communicate that message. Every child grows up within a culture, and we all are part of culture. We shall now focus on the cultural level of language, where we see language being used for cultural manifestation.

In every culture, you will find that, at a certain age before the children grow up to be adults, they are taught how to use language properly; how to debate with one another; how to speak properly; how to become good orators and so on. This, in our own culture, would be enhanced by telling riddles; telling stories and so on. It is in this process also that the society develops its own cultural achievements which indicate how far it has been able to move and to manifest also its own world-view.

So, the Greeks for instance, have as part of their culture considerable literature, myths and legends which are very elaborate, When you look at these and the other things that the Greeks were able to achieve, including their religion, you will find that it is very much related to the way they used their language.

The third level of language as technology is perhaps the most important of all, when we talk about the Christian message. It is at the level of intellectual discipline where we learn to be responsible in the use of language. We discriminate in what we ought to say; what we think we ought to do and what we think we ought not to do. At lower levels, we may not be able to do so; but at this level, we learn how to say what we want to say and how not to say it, depending on the relevant circumstances.

We learn to translate concepts from one language to another; from one pillar to the next; from one section of the society to the other. We also learn to relate ideas with one another; and we also learn to analyse logically as we are trying to do in this book as well as to systematize, to organize our ideas and our concepts into systems.

Let us now assume that our message has been cummunicated and we have got across to the recipient or the receiver. If we are talking in purely technical terms, our main concern is to make sure that we understand the make of the receiver that we are using, know the model that is being used, its capacity; that is, the wattage and all the other specifications that the experts talk about. We need those specifications because without them it will not be possible for us to tune in properly. And of course we have to be aware of the cost of the purchase, the cost of installation and the cost of maintenance.

Now, we are not talking about transmitting from a transmitting station. We are talking about communicating the Christian message. But these analogies apply just as well. If we want the message to reach the recipient, we have also to ask ourselves these quetions. So, we have to concern ourselves with the social specifications of the recipient. We have to know the culture, if you want you may call that the *make, the brand* name and the language that is spoken. We need to understand it thoroughly because if we do not, we are likely to get into a situation where we think we are communicating the message when, in fact, we are not. In one case, for instance, the word adultery, in Gikuyu (Gutharia) and the word for destroying a roof (Gutharia) are spelt the same but pronounced differently. It would cause a great misunderstanding and embarrassment if one word was exchanged for the other.

So for someone who does not understand the exact context in which the word is being used, one may think that one is communicating, while there is no communication at all. It is also possible, if the language is not thoroughly understood, for the opposite of what is intended to be communicated.

The education of the recipient is also extremely important, and by education I do not mean schooling. Rather I am using the word to mean the socialization process. That is, the process by which an individual is helped to become an adult, a responsible, mature member of his society. That will have to be taken care of and thoroughly understood if the communication process is going to be successful. So, also, will the interests of the recipient and the needs of the recipient — the primary and the secondary as well as the higher needs which we might call the tertiary needs, the intellectual and the spiritual needs of the person.

Conversion and Acculturation

Perhaps we need to use familiar terms in Christian literature. What we want of the recipient is to convert him. I consider it worthwhile for us to examine these notions of conversion and acculturation more closely.

These two concepts are closely related but not identical. There is the prosess of *conversion* and there is also the process of *acculturation*. Unfortunately, conversion and acculturation have tended to be used inter-changeably. It is very important to distinguish between them. *Conversion* is a shift from one belief system or one value system to another. *Acculturation* on the other hand is the incorporation into or the adoption of a foreign cultural tradition. Now, if one is communicating the Christian message, coming from one culture to people of another culture, it is possible for him to be acculturating others into his own cultural system and not converting the people at all. When Jesus talks about the Christian mission, about propagating the Good News, he is not talking about acculturation — he is talking about *conversion*. The question that we have to ask ourselves is how we can go about this project of Christian mission in such a way that the people we are reaching end up with conversion, and not acculturation.

Now, how can this be achieved? For the sake of illustration, let us take two individuals — one is a West European (and with West European, I include here the North American and also the Australian and the New Zealand people who have come from the cultures of Western Europe) and one an African. From what we have covered so far, it should be clear by now that the individual is not an isolated atom within the social environment. He is the product of a social system. That system is built up of the pillars that we have already referred to, including the world-view and the basic values of that society. He also has to operate within the social structures which are built in the context of that world-view. As an individual, certain practices are expected of him so that, if he does not do them, it is known that something is wrong.

Christianity as a universal religion is a movement which has been built from three systems, three complete systems each of which had the five cultural pillars that we talked about — the Hebrew culture, the Greek culture and the Latin culture. But, when it was built, it was built in such a way that its link with the Western world-view, became very obvious and very strong. In the formulation of what we now call the basic Christian creeds, the philosophy that is presupposed in those creeds is very strongly Graeco-Roman.

The philosophy underlying the doctrine of trinity can be traced back to the philosophy of Plato through Plotinus. Therefore, it is a philosophy which has its background in the very strong cultural roots of the Western intellectual tradition. As a consequence, the West European's link with Christianity, his practices, his social structures and his world-view pose no problem at all. He is quite at home in contrast with his African counterpart.

But when you take the African individual, what happens? Well, Christianity was preached to him. The fact in history and in sociology is that the Africans themselves have not, in fact, been totally forced to accept the Christian message. They have actually accepted it and the role of the foreign missionary has been to preach to a few people in a mission station. Those people have gone and spread the Word, and some converts themselves have willingly accepted the Word. So Christianity has had its own force of attraction. But, at the same time, the African has become associated, has identified himself, with the social structures and the practices of the culture of the missionary who has introduced the Christian message to him.

At this level, the pressures of the social structures and the social practices of the people who have introduced Christianity have been brought to bear on the African individual. But only the practices and the social structures have had an impact. The basic world-view and the basic values of the West, the African has hardly been willing to internalize. Until the present time, very few African Christians internalized the cultural and philosophical roots of the thing called "Western Christianity."

We have already referred to the gospel of John, chapter 1 verse 1, as a case in point. "In the beginning was the Word, and the Word was with God and the Word was God". What kind of language is that? What is one talking about? It seems nonsensical. Unless one really understands the cultureal process that we talked about earlier, it does not really make sense without a proper translation. And when you take the message from the English language and you translate it into an African language, it becomes even more nonsensical, even more bewildering.

To be able to understand the message, you are compelled to go back to Greek and Hebrew — to the mind of the person who was writing the passage, and so to bypass the English language in order to get that message. Now, how many of us have got the facility to read Greek and Hebrew? Very few. How many people have got the time to go and read those commentaries in order to understand that the Word they are reading about is *Logos?* According to ancient Greek thinking, the world was not brought about by a person or a god who created it. The world was put together by a rational principle such that everything fits within that order. The writer of John's gospel is trying to bring together two different traditions, two world-views, and he is suggesting to the Greeks that the principle called *Logos* is the same reality which the Hebrews call *YHWH.* But that does not at all come clearly in that English passage: "In the beginning was the Word and the Word was with God and the Word was God."

The problem is, how else could the writers of the King James version express that verse? How could they translate it? Those "primitive" Englishmen did not think of their world as having come into being in that way at all. Yet they had to translate the scriptures. And so this passage remains obscure in English. But to the writer of John's gospel it was very relevant and meaningful.

As we pointed out, the West European individual has an advantage because there is a very strong link between Christianity and his whole world-view and social structures. For the African there is a gap. There is not even a remote connection as we have with the Western world-view. There is a total gap.

Between the basic African world-view and the value system on the one hand and Christianity on the other, the link is just not there. I am suggesting that for conversion to take place, there ought *not* to be that gap. There has to be a very strong link between Christianity and the world-view of the African. This is not an easy exercise. But it is not too difficult either, if we begin to analyse what it means for us to be Christians as Africans with our own social heritage, with our own cultural heritage, with our own religious heritage. It may mean looking at the whole of the Christian message again. We shall have to go far enough until we begin to ask these questions — to ask as the writer of John's gospel was asking: What does it mean for a Greek person to become a Christian? What is the relationship between him and the Hebrew? What is the relationship between myself as an African Christian and a European Christian?

The fact that my expression of the Christian faith is going to be different from that of the expression of some friend of mine who is a Canadian or a Chinese is not a negative thing. That is what is so fascinating about the Christian faith — that we can say different things and that the Christian faith can make sense in so many different ways and yet we affirm the brotherhood and the sisterhood of all of us and the providence of God.

I would suggest that if the gospel was not universal in its appeal; if it was not so universal, then it is not the Gospel and I have no need of it. Then I could remain with my own culture. But if it can help me to have life and have it more fully as an African while it helps somebody else in another culture thousands of miles away, then ha! it must really be fascinating. It is something even worth dying for. But then we have talked about this process of conversion and acculturation — how does one really go about it? Several models are possible.

Models of Conversion and Acculturation

The diagram on conversion and acculturation (see appendix) shows that you could have a conversion and an acculturation process which did not take care of the world-view at all. In that case you would only have social structures and practices alone. The individual behaviour of the person would derive from only the social structures and practices. That kind of life would be very superficial because it would not touch the deep roots of the African individual or of any other individual for that matter. Behaviour which is not founded on the basic value system and basic world-view remains very superficial.

Complete conversion should affect all the four components we have talked about earlier — basic world-view, basic value system, social structures and practices.

In the acculturation process, several attempts and methods have been used. One is that of absorption where, for instance, the new and more powerful culture wants to absorb the native ones. It may be done by *indoctrination* as happened, for instance, when the Holy Roman Empire was being built; when the church wanted to regard itself as an empire. You indoctrinate everybody and then incorporate them in that way; or it can be done through *assimilation* as happened in the French colonial system where the aim was to absorb the colonial subjects into the imperial culture.

Yet another model is that of *evolution* in which the *powerful* culture would want to "help" the *weaker* culture so that its members grow gradually until such a time as they become "civilized", having "grown" to a level where they themselves can be considered complete gentlemen, "completely civilized." Such was the method of the Belgian colonial system. Yet another model would be one of *separation,* in which it would be considered better not to try to tamper with the cultures: let each one develop on its own as, for instance, was tried in the "dual mandate" of the British colonial system in Africa. Each community would develop on its own and then there would be no need for any friction between them. One version of that approach was that of *exclusion* in which the invading culture asserted itself and, in spite of its having come to a new environment, wanted to *exclude* everybody else and suggest that everybody else is really not a human being, is not a full human being. The most extreme form of that approach is *apartheid,* which is a system of exclusion with the rulers alone reserving the right of admission.

The fourth option would be *annihilation* — total destruction which would suggest that if the new culture was not willing to adjust itself, to adapt itself, to incorporate itself into the demands of the powerful one, then it would be destroyed. For instance, this happened in the earlier days of the spread of Islam from Arabia across North Africa to Europe. If the Muslim expansion had not been checked in the 11th century, as the Moslems were crossing Spain, the whole of Europe today would be Islamic without doubt because either you submitted or you were destroyed; and the limit would be the power — as long as the invader was strong, it would either subdue or annihilate.

The fifth model is what I would call *nurture/education.* This would work only in a setting in which the parents or members of the present generation would already have accepted the culture and they would be indoctrinating, training their offspring to accept the new culture or religion.

This approach is possible of course with adults, but it is much more difficult than with children because of the variables of socialization. In both conversion and acculturation, these models are applicable. Exclusion and separation are common in mission. Some people think that they are holier than others and operate missionary work on that assumption in spite of the condemnation of that attitude by Jesus.

There is also the model of *proselytization* which is really a method of incorporation, suggesting that people who claim to have the *message* and the *culture* are the ones to determine the norms by which everybody else should be converted. Such was the method used by the Jews, and those Gentiles who wanted to become Jews would have to be proselytized, not converted. They would have to undergo the cultural rituals that would make someone a second-class Jew in order that they would have the permission to be called Jews. The temple in Jerusalem had a court for the Jews and a court for the Gentiles. But they would not be just any Gentiles. It would be those Gentiles who would have been proselytized. So *apartheid* would remain within the Church structures themselves.

The very first Ecumenical Council that is documented in history was over this question — the question as to the ideal model of conversion. The Jewish Christians (some of them) felt that in order for the Gentiles to be admitted into the Church, they should undergo the ritual of becoming a Jew.

Paul was very adamant with his very powerful tools of analysis. He was very keen to sugggest that the Christian faith was a totally new kind of message and that it was not necessary for anyone to be proselytized in order to become a Christian. In Christ, there is neither a Jew nor a Gentile, neither male nor female, neither master nor slave because all are one.

The nurture/education approach is commendable in Christianity. The *encounter and response* model is uniquely appropriate. God meets us and we respond — as Paul on the road to Damascus, and others who have had that kind of conversion experience in which God meets us, whoever we are, wherever we are, and we respond and that becomes an effective method of conversion.

Finally, there is what I would call *evangelization,* which is a process and not an event. It is a process of communicating the Christian message effectively, patiently, and constructively. That is the method that I myself advocate, and it is what this whole book is about. The process of communicating the Christian message is not just a matter of going to bubble some words in the hope that somebody else is going to listen to them and accept them. It is a much more complicated process.

The Impact of Mission

We are in the final stage of our discussion where we should look at the impact of mission. What is it that we expect to achieve? In our assessment, we could use quantitative indicators. For instance, we could look at the actual achievement that has already been attained or that is expected to be attained. It is possible to say: So many Bibles have been distributed in a certain area; or we expect by the year X to have distributed so many bibles; so many schools to have been constructed. You could expect, in quantitative terms, by a certain period to have constructed so many primary schools, secondary schools, colleges and so on. You could expect to have sunk so many wells, established so many clinics and so on. You could also expect to have constructed so many places of worship in a certain area by a given time. Or looking back in time, you could count how many had been constructed. You could expect to recruit or welcome more members in to the Church. These are examples of quantitative indicators.

But it is also possible to assess the impact in terms of quality, which is more difficult. The indicators used when you are concerned about quality are not in terms of tangible things. They are in terms of ideals. They refer to qualitative change in the conduct and expectation of the individual. These are much more difficult to measure, but they are much more important. We have observed earlier that Africa lacks ideals towards which its people could direct their individual aspirations and cultural goals.

Here for the sake of illustration and in the context of our own situation, I would say that when we in Kenya talk about Peace, Love and Unity, these are not quantitative but qualitative indicators. They are ideals. As a Christian, one might be able to appreciate these indicators through study and analysis of the scriptures. It is possible to relate these ideals, for instance, to St. Paul's teaching on faith, hope and love. It is also possible to relate them to participation, sustainability and justice.

The most valuable assessment of the impact of mission is at the level of ideals, at the level of expectations. This level is also the most difficult. It could easily happen that when you have a very great success quantitatively, you may not necessarily be achieving what you intended to achieve qualitatively. For instance, you may build many educational centres, many clinics. You teach many men and women about many methods of contraception. The aim is that families become happier; that parents have more time with their children; that children have got more resources from their parents so that they can get more education; and more material benefits in society. But the quantitative achievements may not be rewarded with qualitative results. The contrary can happen.

Now, one would hope that when quantitative indicators are used, one may be able to note that very many educational centres have been built; very much more literature has been distributed; many more people have been reached. But in qualitative terms, are the families who have been reached happier? Do the parents have more time with their children and so on? It might be shocking to find that the attainment of material success did not necessarily lead to the attainment of qualitative success.

The suggestion here is that the gospel is about the attainment of qualitative goals, not the achievement of quantitative success. In our own work, we ought to concentrate our attention on the qualitative impact of whatever we do without, of course, neglecting the material aspects. But the quantitative indicators should only be as a service in order to attain the qualitative ideals which we are hoping for. This is the eschatological dimension of Christian evangelization.

NOTES

1. For an extended discussion of this insight, see J.N.K, Mugambi, *African Christian Theology: An East African Perspective, op.cit.*

2. A detailed elaboration of this view of cultures is presented in J.N.K. Mugambi, *The African Heritage and Contemporary Christianity, op.cit.*

3. For detailed discussion of the role of language in culture, see J.N.K. Mugambi, "Discernment of Meaning in Discourse with Reference to Religion", Ph.D. Thesis, University of Nairobi, 1983.

4. Various aspects of this theme are discussed and documented in M. Kranzberg and W.H. Davenport, eds., *Technology and Culture: An Anthology,* New York: New American Library, 1972. The approach in this chapter is quite different and this author finds it more realistic and relevant for the analysis in this book.

5. For further discussion of the distinction between conversion and acculturation, see J.N.K. Mugambi, "Some Perspectives of Christianity in Context of the Modern Missionary Enterprise", *op.cit.;* J.N.K. Mugambi, *The African Heritage and Contemporary Christianity, op.cit.*

NOTES

Appendices

BEING THE CHURCH TODAY

1. The Challenge — Mission

2. The Dynamics of Mission — Interactions

3. The Message of Mission — Healing in Wholeness

4. The Medium of Mission
   — Language
   — Channels
   — Links
   — Social Environment

5. The Receiver/Recipient/Receptor in Mission

6. The Impact of Mission
   — Intended Impact (Ideal)
   — Actual Impact

7. Self-Critical Evaluation

APPENDIX 2

THE PRIMARY TASK OF THE CHURCH

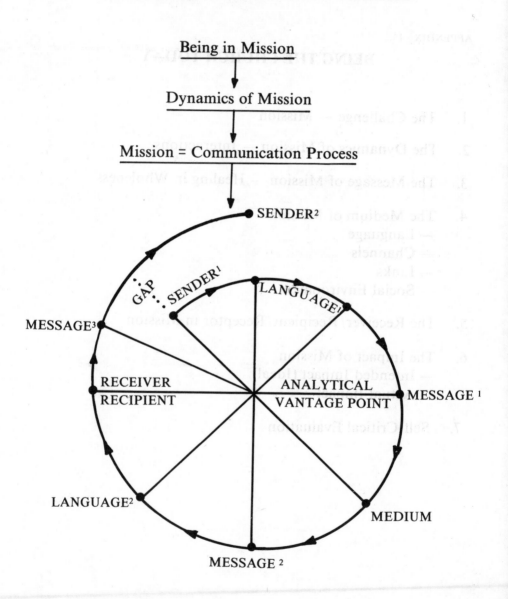

Being in Mission

↓

Dynamics of Mission

↓

Mission = Communication Process

THE MESSAGE OF MISSION

SENDER = GOD
MESSAGE = GOOD NEWS

WHOLESOME HEALING

THEORY
Economics
Ethics
Politics
Aesthetics
Metaphysics

SOCIAL
STRUCTURES

PRACTICE
Wholesome Healing of
Individual and Society —
Physical
Mental
Emotional
Intellectual

IDEOLOGY   THEOLOGY   RITUAL

FAITH   HOPE   LOVE

PARTICIPATION   SUSTAINABILITY   JUSTICE

LIBERATION — SALVATION

GOOD NEWS   =   ULTIMATE FULFILMENT

APPENDIX 4

THE MEDIUM OF MISSION

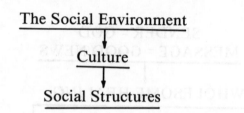

The Social Environment

↓

Culture

↓

Social Structures

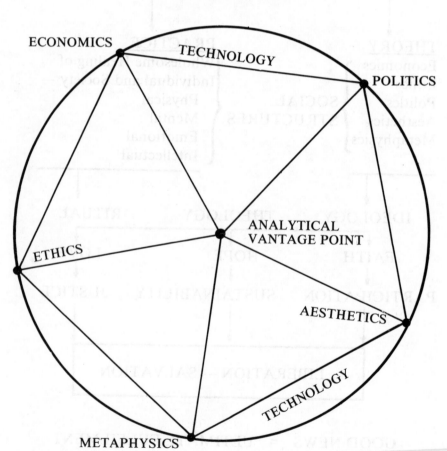

TECHNOLOGY

Technology = *Logos* about *Techne*
            = Organised Knowledge about Tools.

            = How to:
            1. Determine the Purpose
            2. Design
            3. Manufacture
            4. Distribute
            5. Diffuse
            6. Install
            7. Operate
            8. Maintain
            9. Replace
            10. Improve

Primary Technology   = Language
                        Nurtural ◄─────────► Cultural

Secondary Technology = 1. Cultural Manifestations
                      = 2. Cultural Achievements

Tertiary Technology   = Intellectual Discipline
                      1. Translation
                      2. Relating of Ideas
                      3. Logical Analysis
                      4. Systematization

APPENDIX 6

RECEIVER/RECIPIENT (RECEPTOR)

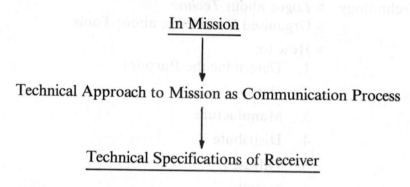

In Mission

Technical Approach to Mission as Communication Process

<u>Technical Specifications of Receiver</u>

1. Make

2. Model

3. Capacity

4. Cost of Purchase, Maintenance and Replacement.

<u>Social Specifications of Recipient/Receptor</u>

1. Culture

2. Language

3. Education (Socialization Process)

4. Interests

5. Needs
    - Primary
    - Secondary
    - Tertiary

CONVERSION AND ACCULTURATION

Conversion   = Shift from One Belief-System (Value System) to another

Acculturation   = Incorporation into, or adoption of a foreign cultural tradition

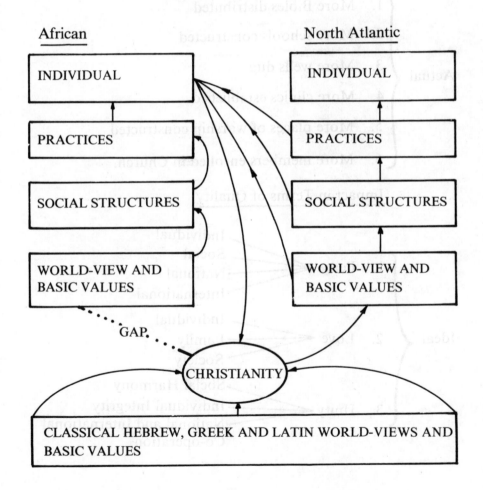

APPENDIX 8

THE IMPACT OF MISSION

Impact in Terms of Quantity

Examples:

Actual
1. More Bibles distributed
2. More schools constructed
3. More wells dug
4. More clinics established
5. More places of worship constructed
6. More members enrolled in Church.

Impact in Terms of Quality

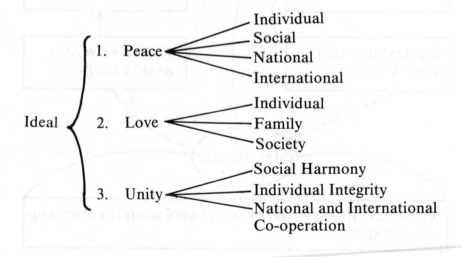

Ideal

1. Peace
   - Individual
   - Social
   - National
   - International

2. Love
   - Individual
   - Family
   - Society

3. Unity
   - Social Harmony
   - Individual Integrity
   - National and International Co-operation

APPENDIX   9

QUESTIONS FOR SELF-CRITICAL EVALUATION

1. What is the main challenge that the church has to meet in response to the needs of Society today?

2. What is the primary task of the church?

3. What is your own denomination doing to meet the challenge?

4. What *is* the emphasis in the actual missionary work of the church today?

5. What *ought to be* the emphasis in the church's missionary work?

6. What *is* the *Message* emphasised by the church in its mission today?

7. What *ought to be* the message?

8. Who are the actual recipients of the message today?

9. Who *ought to be* the recipients?

10. Assess the overall impact of mission today?

Index

Abolitionist Movement 80
Acculturation 124ff
Acts of the Apostles 12
Adler, E. 51
Aesthetics 116
African:
    Christian Theology 3, 17, 36, 105
    Theologians 3, 22, 23
    Theology 4
    Converts 9
    Cultures 9
    Ontological System 27
    Charismatic Churches 86
    Missionaries 87
Agricultural Programmes 67
Alexandria 77
All Africa Conference of Churches (ii)
Allen, R. 119
Analysis and Synthesis 69, 74
Anderson, W.B. 21
Anglican:
    Catechism 92ff
    Communion 98
Anti-Colonial Struggle 83
Antioch 59
Apartheid 79
Appiah-Kubi, K. 68
Appocryphal Books 5
Aristotle 80
Asia Minor 59
Athanasius 92
Augustine 82

Baptism and Naming 92ff
Barrett D.B. 20, 57, 83, 90
Barth, K. 24, 33
Beaver, R.P. 108
Beetham, T.A. 57

Berlin:
    Conference 79
    Treaty 79
Bible 5, 6, 7, 11, 32, 33, 34
Bismark 79
Boecker, H.J. 50, 51
Bonhoeffer, D. 35, 38, 40, 50, 67
British Missionary Societies 82
Brown, C. 24, 35, 37, 38
Buddha 5
Bultmann, R. 34, 38, 67

Captivity 41
Carcopino, J. 77, 89
Carthaginians 77
Catholic Higher Institute of Eastern
    Africa 75
China 77, 79
Chipenda, J. (ii)
Christian Liberty 49
Church 12, 13, 52, 53
Circumcision 15, 16
Clement 92
Collier, G. (iv)
Commission for Higher Education 108
Conceptual Tools 69, 73
Cone, J.H. 37, 90
Conn, C.P. 109
Constantine, Emperor, 12, 39
Contextuality 7
Conversion 124ff
Copernicus 30
Coptic Church 12
Corinth 25
Corporate Responsibility 14
Counter-Reformation 59
Creation, Doctrine of 10
Crisis of Authority in Mission (i)

Cultural Traditions 9
Curriculum Development 69, 75

Dark Ages 12, 50
Darwin, C. 30, 31
Data Exchange 66
Davenport, W.H., 131
Deductive Logic 26
Denominational Competition 17
Discipleship 8, 10, 11, 13, 14, 40
Division of World Mission and
        Evangelism (i), 61
Doctrinal Controversies 6
Dogma 10
Donatist Schism 78
Donders, J.G. 38
Durham (iv)

Eastern Orthodoxy 59
Economics 116
Ecumenical:
  Movement (ii), 32, 39, 62, 65, 66, 67
    68, 87
  Sharing of Resources (ii), (iii), 58, 59
Egypt 59, 77
Einstein, A. 67
Energy 67
Environment 67
Erasmus 104
Estrangement from God 41
Ethics 116
Ethiopia 59
European Culture 18
Evangelical Revivals 82
Evans, R. (iii)
Evolution 10, 30

Faith 118
Fisher, H.A.L. 50, 88
Free-Will 28
Freedom 40, 43, 44
Fuller, R. 19

Galatians 14
Gentiles 15
Georgis 81
Ghana 84, 85
Gifford, P. 109
Good News 7, 10, 13, 45, 56, 62, 63,
    88, 110
Gothic Architecture 12
Gregorian University 2

Hardy, E.R. 50
Hartford Theological Seminary (ii)
Harvey, W. 30
Health Programmes 66
Hinduism 5
Hobbes, T. 104
Hope 39, 40, 118
Howell, L. 50, 109
Hughes, P. 20, 68
Human Dignity 44

Illness 41
Impact of Mission 129ff
Independent Churches 6, 18, 56, 115
India 77, 79
Inductive Reasoning 28
International Trávelling Seminars (i),
    (ii)
Isaiah 42
Islam 5, 87
Ismaily, A.K. (iv)

James, E.O. 20
Jerusalem, Council of 14, 15, 18, 49
Jesus 5, 7, 8, 25, 39, 45
Jews 15, 59
John the Baptist 8, 15, 40, 41
Johnson, P. 80, 90
Judaism 5, 14, 15, 16, 25, 43
Justice 40, 44, 116
Justification by faith 6

Kant, I. 67
Kendall, E. 90, 108, 109
Kenya 56
King, K.J. 90, 108
Kingdom of God 9, 13, 18, 19, 26,
   41, 44, 46
Kings, G. (iv)
Kraemer, H. 90
Kranzenberg M. 131

Language 121ff
Lean, G. 90
Lefever, E.W. 109
Liberation 56, 84, 86, 119
Lima 60
Literacy 17
Livingstone, D. 81, 109
Local Church 22
Locke, J. 104
Lorimer, E.O. 89
Love 25, 118
Luther, M. 6, 59
Lutheranism 80
Lyall, L. 88, 91, 109

Margull, H.J. 50
May, H.G. 20
Mbiti, J.S. 20, 24, 29, 37, 102, 103,
   108, 109
McCormick Theological Seminary (iii)
McGowen C.H. 38
Messiah 40
Metaphysical 116
Metzger B.M. 20
Middle Ages 6, 80
Miller, P. 76
Mission Fields 64
Missionary Societies 12
Modern:
   Ecumenical Movement 23
   Missionary Enterprise 17, 18, 60,
      62, 83, 84

Missionary Movement 16, 60, 81
Maratorium Debate 63
More, T. 104
Muga, E. 20
Mugambi, J.N.K. 20, 38, 67, 109, 119,
   131
Muin, S. (ii)
Muller-Fahrenholz, G. (iii)
Mutual:
   Consultancy 64
   Exchange 64
Mwaniki, H.S.K. 89
Mythical Literature 10
Myths 9, 34
Mzimela, S. 89

Nairobi Assembly 62
National:
   Council of Churches of Kenya (ii), 3
   Councils of Churches 66
Nazareth 7
Neill, S.C. 78, 82, 87, 88, 89, 90, 91
New-Delhi (I), 61
New Ecclesiology 60
New Hermennentics 60
New Reformation 60
New Testament 5, 7, 10, 13, 58, 119
Newbigin, L. 67
Ngulukulu (iv)
Nicodemus 42
Nkrumah K. 84

Ochieng' W. 89
Odeng' R. (ii)
Oduyoye, M. 90
Old Testament 5, 40, 99, 119
Oliver, R. 1, 2, 90, 103, 108, 109
Omari, B. (iv)
Oppression 41, 44
Orientation, 64

Participation 118
Paul, St.   6, 13, 25, 45, 107
Peace   40, 130
People of God   47
Pharisees   5, 83
Pietism   83
Pilgrims   10
Pilkington, R.   20
Politics   116
Polkinghorne J.   20
Positivism   10
Poverty   41
Prejudice   41, 42, 43
Programme to Combat Racism   49, 56
Proselytes   14, 15
Protestant:
   Churches   5
   Denominations   7
   Tradition   5
Puritans   79

Qu'ran   5
Quintero, M.   (ii)

Reconciliation   40, 44
Reformation   5, 6, 59, 84
Reformed Christianity   39
Relief Work   57
Religious Education   69, 76
Research and Development   65
Revelation   24, 27, 28, 36, 39
Richardson, A.   108
Roman Province of Africa   77
Rousseau, J.J.   27, 104
Russel, B.   30, 37, 38, 89

Salvation   6
Samaritan   11, 25, 43
Saul   59
Scholarship Programme   63
Scientific Theory   10
Scribes   5

Secularism   82
Slave Trade   80, 82
Smart, N.   19
Social Context of Christianity   (iii)
Social Dimension of Mission   9
South Africa   42, 56
Spain   77, 78
Sundkler, B.   57
Survival   44
Sustainability   118

Tambaram   60
Taylor, J.V.   17
Tempels, P.   37
Theological Maturity   2
Theology of Oppression   56
Thessalonica   25
Third WCC Assembly   (i)
Thomas Aquinas   80
Tillich, P.   67, 76, 108, 109
Timothy   25
Torah   5
Torres, S.   68
Training   63
Trajan, Emperor   78
Trent, Council of   59, 61

Unity   40, 130
Universal Principles   25
Universities   66
Untouchables   42
Upper Nile   77
Uppsala   60

Values   106, 107
Van der Bent, A.J.   51
Vatican   II 60, 61
Vedas   5
Vernaculars   6
Violence   43
Vischer, L.   (iii)
Vissert' Hooft W   50

Were, G.S.   89
Western Theology   36
Williams C.   77, 89
Williams E.   90
Wilmore, G.S.   37
Word of God   34
Works   6
World Council of Churches   (i), (ii),
    (iii), 40, 49, 50, 51, 56, 60, 61, 63,
    93, 100
World Missionary Conference   60
World Student Christian
    Federation   (ii)
Wright, G.E.   19

Yoder, H.   50

Zacchaeus   42
Zealots   44
Zimbabwe   56
Zorn, H.M.   76